The Aztec Pantheon and the Art of Empire

THE
AZTEC PANTHEON

AND THE
ART OF EMPIRE

JOHN M. D. POHL and CLAIRE L. LYONS

The J. Paul Getty Museum
Los Angeles

Getty Publications
1200 Getty Center Drive, Suite 500
Los Angeles, CA 90049-1682
www.getty.edu/publications

This publication is issued in conjunction with the exhibition *The Aztec Pantheon and the Art of Empire*, on view in the J. Paul Getty Museum at the Getty Villa in Malibu, from March 24 through July 5, 2010.

Gregory M. Britton PUBLISHER

Beatrice Hohenegger EDITOR
Stuart Smith DESIGNER
Suzanne Watson PRODUCTION COORDINATOR
Holly Ortiz PHOTO RESEARCHER

Printed in China

Library of Congress Cataloging-in-Publication Data
Pohl, John M. D.
  The Aztec pantheon and the art of empire / John M.D. Pohl and Claire L. Lyons.
    p. cm.
  "This publication is issued in conjunction with the exhibition, The Aztec Pantheon and the Art of Empire, on view in the J. Paul Getty Museum at the Getty Villa in Malibu, from March 24 through July 5, 2010"—T.p. verso.
  Includes bibliographical references and index.
  ISBN 978-1-60606-007-0 (hardcover)
1. Aztecs—Religion—Exhibitions. 2. Aztec gods in art—Exhibitions. 3. Aztec sculpture—Exhibitions. 4. Rome—Religion—Exhibitions. 5. Gods, Roman, in art—Exhibitions. 6. Gods, Greek, in art—Exhibitions. 7. Syncretism (Religion)—Mexico—Exhibitions. 8. Mexico—History—Conquest, 1519–1540—Religious aspects—Exhibitions. I. Lyons, Claire L., 1955– II. Title.
 F1219.76.R45P64 2010
 299.7'8452—dc22
                2009037555

Front Cover: Detail of Plate XIII, Incense Burner with Chicomecoatl, from Tlahuac, Mexico City, 1325–1521, H 105 × W 72 × D 48.5 cm (42 × 28¾ × 18¼ in.), Museo Nacional de Antropología, Mexico City, 10–571544

Page III: Detail of Plate XXXIII, *Ehecatl-Quetzalcoatl*, found in Calixtlahuaca, About 1500, Basalt and pigment, H 176 × W 56 × D 50 cm (69¼ × 22 × 19⅝ in.), Museo de Antropología e Historia del Estado de México, Toluca, 10–109262

Back Cover: Syllabary of sacred hearts, Nahuatl pictographs and the Roman alphabet, Diego Valadés (Mexican, 1533–after 1582), in Diego Valadés, *Rhetorica christiana…* (Christian Rhetoric…), Perugia, 1579, plate at p. 100; H 19 × W 12.7 cm (7½ × 5 in.). Research Library, the Getty Research Institute, 1388-209.

Contents

Forewords

THE AZTEC *Pantheon and the Art of Empire* is a landmark exhibition for the J. Paul Getty Museum. In the early 1980s, when the Getty Board of Trustees decided to redevelop the Getty Villa and dedicate it to the display of Greek, Roman, and Etruscan antiquities, plans were also set into motion to broaden its mission to include the comparative study of ancient cultures. After I assumed my position as Director of the Getty Museum in late 2005, right before the Villa was reopened, I decided to make the inclusion of works of art into our exhibition program from outside the classical Mediterranean world and the European tradition a fundamental priority. At the same time, the Getty had long nurtured a deep interest both in the afterlife of antiquity in the modern period and in the cultural exchanges between Europe and Latin America.

When considering the possibilities for comparative archaeology at the Getty Villa, Mexico's unique artistic heritage stood out as a logical and inspiring choice for our first such project. It is important to remember that the Renaissance rediscovery of Graeco-Roman antiquity coincided with the exploration and colonization of the Americas, and that analogies were inevitably drawn between two great empires—the Aztec and the Roman—as Europeans confronted the revelations of the New World in the pursuit of an imperial mission. In turn, their encounter with hitherto unknown civilizations kindled fresh interest in Europe's own ancient past.

The Aztec Pantheon thus offers an ideal opportunity to explore the potential of comparative archaeology by displaying outstanding examples of Mexico's pre-Hispanic artistic heritage in the classical setting of the Getty Villa. It is especially gratifying to be able to schedule this exhibition in 2010, when both the bicentennial of Mexican independence and the centennial of the Mexican Revolution will be celebrated with special interest by the Mexican community of Los Angeles. We are delighted our Aztec project will be part of a broader cultural initiative being undertaken across southern California to mount exhibitions, performances, and public programs to commemorate this milestone in Mexican history.

Many colleagues in Mexico have been generous partners and our thanks go out to them for lending these precious works of art. At the inception of the project, Alfonso de Maria y Campos, director general of the National Institute of Anthropology and History (INAH), and Consuelo Sáizar, president of the National Council for Culture and the Arts (CONACULTA), extended timely offers of cooperation. We are deeply saddened that the late Felipe Solís Olguín, the former director of the Museo Nacional de Antropología in Mexico City, whose encouragement at an early stage in the planning helped shape our ideas so positively, did not live to see this exhibition. I must acknowledge the contributions of his successor, Dr. Diana Magaloni Kerpel, and to Carlos Gonzáles Gonzáles, director of the Museo del Templo Mayor, without whose support the project could not have been brought to such a fruitful conclusion. We are also most grateful to Franca Arduini, former Director of the Biblioteca Medicea Laurenziana in Florence, and to her successor, Maria Prunai Falciani, for agreeing to lend a volume of the splendid Florentine Codex, a unique chronicle of Aztec culture that returns to the "New World" for the first time in more than four centuries. At the Getty Museum, I would like to thank Karol Wight, senior curator of Antiquities, and Claire Lyons, curator of Antiquities, together with John Pohl, adjunct professor in the Department of Art History at the University of California, Los Angeles, for transforming a challenging concept into an original and provocative display for our Villa visitors. The tremendous success of *The Aztec Pantheon and the Art of Empire* has inspired us all to think even more broadly about future collaborative projects, which we anticipate will bring to the Getty galleries exceptional works of art from around the world along with new research, analysis, and interpretation.

Michael Brand
Director, The J. Paul Getty Museum

HISTORY, a discipline that offers an account of human events, has found different ways to describe and explain *power* and *dominion* as phenomena that are continually repeated in different periods and places. Because the Graeco-Roman tradition is one of the fundamental sources through which the West understands history, it is no accident that when the Spaniards arrived on this continent, they attempted to explain its inhabitants from within their own parameters. Having battled the Moors, some compared the Aztec with the Ottoman empire, while others associated Tenochtitlan, their splendid city surrounded by lakes, with cosmopolitan Venice. Still others, learning of the dizzying speed with which the Aztecs emerged and were consolidated as the dominant power in Mesoamerica, equated them with the Roman empire.

This last analogy found great success, for it was also fueled by the ongoing creation of universal symbols introduced by the Jesuits during the fifteenth and sixteenth centuries, with the express intent to build, throughout the hemisphere, a world civilization based on the values of Christianity and on Roman tradition. Teachers to generations of thinkers and politicians, the Jesuits instilled in the Creole population a pride in their own Mexican roots. From the outset, however, these roots were understood from a Roman perspective—the sacred world of the Aztecs was organized in a similar way to the Graeco-Roman pantheon, and their nobles were understood as sharing interests with the patrician classes.

For much of the nineteenth century this paradigm remained in use. Suffice it to remember that during the Mexican neoclassical period, artists recreated the pre-Hispanic world in the architectonic and even anatomical forms of ancient Greece and Rome. Even during the twentieth century, the chronological framework in which pre-Columbian Mesoamerica was studied—preclassical, classical (referring to the splendor of Maya civilization, which in the eyes of early scholars was similar to the Greek *polis*), and post-classical—clearly reveals an ancient Mediterranean debt.

We are grateful to the curators of the J. Paul Getty Museum not only for the opportunity to historicize this way of viewing ancient Mexico, but also for analyzing a frankly interesting hypothesis: the existence of historical and rhetorical modes in the establishment of imperial domains that, independent of the cultural horizon from which peoples originate, are similar throughout the world.

The National Institute of Anthropology and History is honored to collaborate on *The Aztec Pantheon and the Art of Empire*, a work both of scientific importance and a celebration of the bicentennial of Independence as well as the centenary of the Mexican Revolution by the people of California, with whom Mexico shares a long common history.

Alfonso de Maria y Campos
Director General
Instituto Nacional de Antropología e Historia

MORE THAN a military conflict, the Conquest of Mexico was a spiritual battle. In *The History of the Indies of New Spain* (1581), Fray Diego Durán described Aztec rituals and divinities as a distortion of ancient western religions: Huitzilopochtli was viewed as a fierce god and the long mythic journey of the Aztecs became a reference to a pilgrimage in search of the Promised Land.

Fray Diego's reasoning is a good example of how the interpretation of the sacred universe of the Aztecs has had a double objective: to approach that which is different in an attempt to understand it and to resituate this entirely unfamiliar cultural reality within parameters comprehensible for westerners.

This is the path that the scholars of ancient Mexico would follow for centuries. During the seventeenth and eighteenth centuries, the Aztec capital Tenochtitlan was compared to imperial Rome in an effort to affirm its splendid past, independent of Spanish roots. The hierarchy of the Aztec deities was thus organized into a pantheon equivalent to that of the sacred world of classical antiquity; and the growth of the Aztec empire—halted only by the arrival of the Europeans—was likened to the precipitous ascent of the Romans.

For these reasons and more, *The Aztec Pantheon and the Art of Empire* at the Getty Villa is important. To help make this exhibition a reality, the Consejo Nacional para la Cultura y las Artes has facilitated loans of masterpieces from a number of Mexican institutions including the National Museum of Anthropology and the Templo Mayor Museum.

Reading history is an act of interpretation. While viewing this exhibition, specialists and visitors alike will enjoy the opportunity to formulate their own interpretations. We invite you to share in the grandeur of these works of art with the profound conviction that the cultural heritage of the Mexican people is the patrimony of all, and that by offering different perspectives, our heritage is transformed into a mirror of the many faces of humanity.

Consuelo Sáizar
President
Consejo Nacional para la Cultura y las Artes
(CONACULTA)

THE *OTHERS*—who are naturally different from *us*—appear before our gaze as an infinite source of curiosity. Moreover, if they are completely unknown to us, their very presence generates in us innumerable questions and sensations that range from unbridled attraction to irrational repulsion. We are immediately overcome with the desire to explicate them, to place them within a frame of reference, and to assign a place to them within our own concept of the universe. And the way to accomplish this, generally speaking, is through analogy. We identify in another those traces that seem familiar and help us construct a bridge between the self and the other, which we call comparison.

As discussed by John Pohl and Claire Lyons in their masterly essay, the Spaniards experienced this type of situation at the dawn of the sixteenth century, when they arrived for the first time in Mesoamerican territory and confronted indigenous societies that had achieved a high level of civilization without outside influence. They found themselves before a reality as unexpected as it was unknown and, in an effort to decipher it, they often reverted to the familiar mirror of contemporary Islam. The Spaniards compared the Mexica and their neighbors with the Moors, infidels they had battled between 711 and 1492—from the time of the Umayyad dynasty to the Taifa kingdoms—during the extensive Reconquest of the Iberian Peninsula. This explains, for instance, why they called the pyramids of Tenochtitlan *mezquitas* (mosques) and their priests *alfaquíes* (religious scholars). It also reveals why evangelization undertaken in the New World followed models applied a few years earlier in the newly subjugated kingdom of Granada.

Even more important to the Spaniards was the model of classical antiquity, mainly that of the Romans. Let us remember that the majority of conquistadors and missionaries were originally from Extremadura and Andalucía, two regions sprinkled with archaeological traces of distant but ever-present Hispania. In fact, many of them had visited the ruins of renamed cities such as Emerita Augusta (Mérida), Corduba (Córdoba), Tarraco (Tarragona), or Itálica (near Seville), the latter the birthplace of emperors Trajan, Hadrian, and Theodosius. The more cultured of them had even read the Latin classics composed by Plutarch, Seneca, Virgil, and many others. Obviously, such familiarity with the past led the Spaniards to automatically link the "polytheists and idolaters" they had just encountered with those of ancient Rome. It is not strange, therefore, that such Mesoamerican deities as Xiuhtecuhtli and Chicomecoatl were understood as "another Vulcan" and "another Ceres," and that Mesoamerican images of domestic worship were called *lares* and *penates*, the household gods of the Romans.

Throughout the colonial period, the classical world continued to be the origin of all sorts of references and comparisons. A graphic example is the construction of the triumphal portal, designed by the celebrated historian of New Spain, Carlos de Sigüenza y Góngora. Erected in Mexico City in 1680, it was an ephemeral structure in the Baroque style that, as opposed to Roman arches, did not welcome victorious emperors but rather "non-bloodthirsty" viceroys, in this case the Marquis of Laguna. Featured at the center of this arch were portraits of the viceroy and vicereine, supported by the images of Mercury and Venus. But in an unusual way, the iconographic program was completed with effigies of Huitzilopochtli and the eleven Mexica emperors, which were associated with an equal number of classical virtues serving as inspiration to the new ruler.

Other examples are the archaeological excavations systematically carried out in Herculaneum, Pompeii, and Stabiae during the eighteenth century, which had profound repercussions in the Hispanic world. In the "metropolis" of Spain, Charles III and Charles IV, as principal promoters of such works, forged an archaizing image of powerful sovereigns and founders of the arts. In New Spain, on the other hand, the excavations awakened in cultured Creole society an interest in local archaeological remains and in the glorious pre-Columbian past, which would in the long run serve as a basis for a new identity and a longing for independence. At the end of the colonial period, Mexica sculptures discovered in the ruins of Tenochtitlan were exhibited side by side with casts of Roman sculptures, including the Laocöon and the Venus de' Medici, at the Academy of San Carlos in Mexico City.

Although of a different kind, the connections persist until today. Just a year ago, the archaeologists of the Templo Mayor Project created a three-dimensional model of the recently unearthed monolith of the Mexica earth goddess Tlaltecuhtli. This would not be noteworthy if it weren't for the fact that we accomplished it in conjunction with our Italian colleagues from the University of Ferrara, who now apply the same scanning techniques in their topographic recording of the famous Via dell'Abbondanza in Pompeii.

Leonardo López Luján
Director of the Proyecto Templo Mayor

Acknowledgments

This book is a companion to the exhibition *The Aztec Pantheon and the Art of Empire* (March 24 to July 5, 2010), organized by the J. Paul Getty Museum. The idea of "parallel pantheons" first took shape in a conversation between Thomas B. F. Cummins, professor of art history at Harvard University, and Getty Museum director Michael Brand. In exploring the implications of parallel pantheons, we realized that from the moment of Europe's first encounters with the Americas, the gods of the Old World were in a dialogue of sorts with those of the New World. Populated by innumerable deities presiding over the forces of nature and tutelary heroes whose mythic deeds gave rise to an all-embracing *cosmovisión*, the Aztec pantheon immediately suggested intriguing comparisons with ancient Mediterranean religions. When Hernán Cortés entered the Valley of Mexico in 1519, he witnessed a cityscape of stupendous architectural monuments, constructed by a highly sophisticated society. Undreamed of except in legends from classical mythology, the Triple Alliance capital at Tenochtitlan had no plausible parallels outside the Roman Empire. Aztec kings ruled over vast tributary territories in central and southern Mexico and enforced their dominion through the machinery of a militaristic, theocratic state. Despite the obvious differences of aesthetics, iconography, and meaning between the exotic cult images of the Aztecs and the figures of the old Roman gods, analogy became a useful tool in the task of cultural translation—and it remains one. Comparative analysis—not only of similarities but also of radical differences—can spark alternative interpretations and encourage new approaches through fresh eyes.

In the context of the neoclassical ambience of the Getty Villa, the presence of masterworks created by Aztec sculptors offers an invaluable chance to experiment—familiarizing visitors with the artistic heritage of Mexico, while at the same time "defamiliarizing" (as Tom Cummins put it) the classical divinities whose statues stand nearby. A Roman bronze eagle, for example, juxtaposed with the powerful basalt eagle *cuauhxicalli*, becomes a metaphor for the function of monumental arts, religious spectacles, and consciously classicizing traditions within empires. Excavations at Roman provincial sites (not least, in Hispania) and in regions outside Mexico City are burgeoning—here the apparent gulf between modes of research can be bridged. Imperialism is a phenomenon that has been filtered by subsequent historical models, including that of the Habsburg court of Charles V, King of Spain and Holy Roman Emperor. Our understanding of the Aztecs has been further complicated by the spirited classical culture that emerged in post-Conquest New Spain—in part due, paradoxically, to the teachings of Franciscan missionaries. Never a one-way export of ideas from Europe to the Americas, one extraordinary consequence of evangelization was the transformation of classical sources by indigenous scholars who articulated their native heritage with European and Christian perspectives to create a dynamic colonial culture on their own terms.

Our own dialogue across the disciplines of anthropology, art history, and classics has been challenging, but the outcome is promising. Intended to introduce aspects of the Aztec pantheon and its reception in Europe to museum visitors, general readers, and specialists alike, this volume presents a series of soundings that raise issues for future exploration. The topic struck an immediate chord with the late Felipe Solís Olguín, director of the Museo Nacional de Antropología in Mexico City. We are especially indebted to him not only for approving major loans but also for his insights, which had a formative influence on the directions we pursued. The notion of parallel pantheons is visualized in the Florentine Codex, an iconic cornerstone of Aztec history, and we express profound thanks to former director Franca Arduini and Maria Prunai Falciani, director of the Biblioteca Medicea Laurenziana in Florence, for granting this unprecedented loan. At the inception of the project, Alfonso de Maria y Campos, director general of the Instituto Nacional de Antropología e Historia (INAH), and Consuelo Sáizar, president of the Consejo Nacional para la Cultura y las Artes, extended a timely offer of cooperation. Diana Magaloni Kerpel, director of the Museo Nacional de Antropología, and Carlos Javier González González, director of the Museo del Templo Mayor, were equally generous in sharing significant works of art and recent archaeological discoveries. We are grateful to Manuel Medina Mora, Salvador Villar, José Ortíz Izquierdo, and Maria del Refugio Cárdenas Ruelas for facilitating the loan of an exceptional painted screen from the collection of the Banco Nacional de México.

Additionally, the exhibition benefited from loans from the Museo de Antropología e Historia del Estado de México, Toluca; Museo Arqueológico de Apaxco; Museo Regional de Puebla; and the Philadelphia Museum of Art. Works of art from these collections join works on paper from the Getty Research Library, and we thank the director, Thomas Gaehtgens, for making rare historical documents available. It has been an exceptional pleasure to collaborate with director Miriam Kaiser and her proficient staff at the Coordinación Nacional de Museos y Exposiciones of the Instituto Nacional de Antropología, notably Leticia Pérez Castellanos, Erika Gómez, and Miguel Angel Báez Pérez, who coordinated the loan procedures so smoothly. Leonardo López Luján, Director of the Proyecto Templo Mayor, kept us appraised of the remarkable discoveries now being made at the Great Temple and shared his deep historical sensibility in the thought-provoking foreword to this volume. Most appreciated was the generous help of Bertina Olmedo Vera, curator of the Sala Mexica at the Museo Nacional de Antropología, and her colleagues Patricia Ochoa Castillo, deputy director, and Laura Filloy Nadal, head of conservation. Fernando Carrizosa Montfort (Museo del Templo Mayor), Gerardo P. Taber (Centro de Estudios de Diversidad Cultural), Martha Gonzalez (CONACULTA), and Pilar Escontrias, formerly at the Fowler Museum at UCLA, also provided much practical assistance. From the beginning, Bertha Cea Echenique, cultural attaché at the U.S. Embassy in Mexico City, was an enthusiastic advocate and expert intermediary. Juan Marcos Guttiérez-González, consul general of Mexico in Los Angeles, and cultural attaché Alejandro Pelayo-Rangel have unstintingly contributed time and support.

Numerous colleagues have been sources of inspiration and constructive advice. We wish to acknowledge Andrew Laird, who joined our cross-disciplinary conversation at the outset and whose innovative research on the classical tradition in Mexico has shaped our thinking. Cecelia Klein, John Pollini, and Khristaan Villela kindly shared their expertise. Thanks to the concerted efforts of a team from across the Getty, the fruits of research materialized and the objects can speak to each other in unexpected ways. Our appreciation is especially due to Michael Brand, Liz Andres, Jacqueline Cabrera, Yve Chavez, John Giurini, Alicia Houtrouw, Paco Link, Rainer Mack, Kevin Marshall, Holly Ortiz, Stuart Smith, Marie Svoboda, Sahar Tchaitchian, Suzanne Watson, Karol Wight, Davina Wolter, and the staff of the exhibitions, design, conservation, education, programming, registrars, communications, and publications departments. Our valiant editor, Beatrice Hohenegger, firmly guided the text into final form, and we thank her for focusing our wide-ranging explorations across centuries and cultures.

Claire L. Lyons and John M. D. Pohl

P a c i f i c
O c e a n

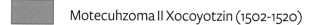 Motecuhzoma II Xocoyotzin (1502-1520)

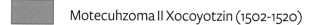 Ahuizotl (1486-1502)

 Tizoc (1481-1486)

 Axayacatl (1469-1481)

 Motecuhzoma Ilhuicamina (1440-1468)

 Izcoatl (1428-1440)

 Independent Territories

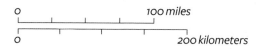

Gulf

of

Mexico

△ Ixmiquilpan

Tula △

Teotihuacan
Azcapotzalco   △
Tlacopan
△△△ TENOCHTITLAN
Tepepulco

Calixtlahuaca △
△ Tlaxcala
Huexotzinco   △ Cacaxtla
△
Cholula

Malinalco △

△ Coixtlahuaca

△ Oaxaca

On August 13, 1521 the last Aztec emperor Cuauhtemoc fled the conflagration of the city of Tenochtitlan by crossing Lake Texcoco toward the western shore. Several months earlier, the bundled effigy of the Aztec patron god Huitzilopochtli had been taken there to insure that, even if the city itself were to fall, the spirit of Cuauhtemoc's people embodied in the holy image would endure. Suddenly the emperor's craft was sighted by a brigantine commanded by the Spanish officer García Holguín. The emperor and his retinue were overtaken, captured, and immediately taken before Hernán Cortés, commander of the combined Spanish-Indian army of more than 150,000 troops that had besieged the city for the past three months. Placing his hand on Cortés's dagger, Cuauhtemoc declared: "I have surely done my duty in defence of my City, and I can do no more and I come by force and a prisoner into your presence and into your power, take that dagger that you have in your belt and kill me at once with it."[1]

Origins and Growth of the Aztec Empire

All around them the imperial capital burned as its last defenders were slaughtered. A putrid stench pervaded the vast metropolis, where the corpses of once valiant warriors had been left to rot in the sun for weeks. By the end of that day, the longest continuous battle in recorded world history came to an end. More than 40,000 lay dead in Tenochtitlan's streets and plazas (**Figure 1**). Cortés assured Cuauhtemoc of his respect for the brilliant defense of the city and guaranteed the safety of the ruler's family. But then, in an extraordinarily dismissive if not bizarre move, the Spanish commander turned away from the Aztec king and proceeded to attend to an argument that had erupted between Holguín and his superior Gonzalo de Sandoval over who should claim credit for Cuauhtemoc's capture. Addressing his disputing captains, Cortés invoked the catastrophic consequences of a rivalry between the ancient Roman generals Gaius Marius and Lucius Cornelius Sulla.[2] Sixteen hundred years earlier, Marius and Sulla had fallen into a bitter personal and political dispute that ultimately pitted the Senate, largely composed of the aristocratic elite, against the Assembly representing the people. The vicious social war of 90 BC that ensued between these factions threatened to destroy the Roman Republic at the height of its prosperity. By equating his captains with two of Rome's most eminent military figures, Cortés's reprimand turned the Spaniards' "civilizing mission" into a historical inevitability. Just like the Romans, whose empire spanned the known world from the shores of the Atlantic Ocean to North Africa and the Middle East, the Spaniard saw themselves as destined to be the rightful "conquistadors" of the New World.

Two inextricably linked objectives motivated the Conquest—acquiring the fabled gold of the Americas and converting the indigenous Mesoamerican population to Christianity. According to a centuries-old tradition extending back to the Muslim domination of the Iberian Peninsula, land could be transferred between individuals according to local custom, but precious metals and minerals planted in the belly of the earth by divine providence were perceived as collective wealth.[3] The consequences of this understanding were profound, empowering entrepreneurial

FIGURE 1 | **The Conquest of Tenochtitlan** | Anonymous | 1650–1700 | Oil on canvas | H 121.9 × W 198.1 cm (48 × 78 in.) | Jay I. Kislak Collection, Library of Congress, Washington, DC | 26.2

conquistadors to act in the name of God while at the same time enriching themselves. A significant percentage of the profits from mining God-given resources was to be invested in the collective welfare of later Christian kingdoms. This portion became the *quinto real*, or "royal fifth," a tax levied by the Crown and administered by God's earthly representative, Charles V, King of Spain and Holy Roman Emperor. Christianity and the royal fifth thereby became the theological and economic foundations on which the conquistadors staked their claim on the Americas.

As Cortés's speech invoking Marius and Sulla makes plain, classical antiquity provided a critical conceptual foundation for the encounter with the peoples of Mesoamerica. Missionaries, militia, and merchants looked to ancient civilizations from Egypt to Persia, the Holy Land, Greece, and Rome as prototypes. Exploration and colonization in the Americas coincided with the Renaissance rediscovery of Graeco-Roman antiquity, and parallels were routinely drawn between two great empires—the Aztec and the Roman. Memories of the Iberian past as Roman Hispania, moreover, were used to forge new understandings of Aztec society as well as to guide and critique the imperial mission. Not simply a dubious imposition by foreign elites, classicism had a formative influence on indigenous and mestizo identities. We perceive the echo of Greek myths and Latin epics in the earliest post-Conquest writings about Aztec culture, as well as in the literature, arts, and festivals celebrated in Mexico during the sixteenth and seventeenth centuries. Contemporary archaeology can be applied to evaluate structural analogies between the imperial states that the Aztecs and the Romans commanded, particularly with regard to the role of monumental art and architecture in political and religious life. This essay considers selected episodes in what was to become a complex three-way dialogue between the Old World, the New World, and the communities that eventually shaped a dual heritage into the unique culture of New Spain.

Though Cuauhtemoc may have understood little of the discourse on Marius and Sulla, he would have comprehended the moral admonition in the tale of the Roman generals' unbridled ambition and the political turmoil it unleashed. Similar histories surrounded the rivalry between the Aztec's ancestral heroes Huitzilopochtli (Hummingbird of the South), Quetzalcoatl (Plumed Serpent), and Tezcatlipoca (Smoking Mirror).

The term "Aztec" is derived from the eponym Aztlan (Place of the White Heron), the homeland of desert Chichimec tribes, who emerged from seven caves located at the heart of a sacred mountain to the northwest of the Valley of Mexico. Divinely inspired to fulfill a destiny of conquest, they journeyed south (**Plate I**).[4] Upon observing a tree struck by a lightning bolt, the seventh and last of these tribes—called the Mexica—took the event as a sign from Huitzilopochtli to follow a separate path. Their wanderings continued for many more years until they eventually settled at the fabled city of Tollan, today identified with the ruins of Tula in the Mexican state of Hidalgo.

By the time of the Spanish Conquest, there were almost as many dramatic performances about the rise of Tollan as there were royal courts in which to enact them. Most stories featured Quetzalcoatl's confrontation with Tezcatlipoca and Huitzilopochtli. Quetzalcoatl taught his people to make the finest jewels, featherwork, textiles, and pottery. Growing rich through the trade in luxury goods, the Toltecs (people of Tollan) allegedly never hungered, for the maize grew as big as grinding stones.[5] Quetzalcoatl opposed human sacrifice, substituting instead offerings of snakes, birds, and butterflies. His cult incurred the ridicule of an opposing faction led by Tezcatlipoca and Huitzilopochtli, rival priests who incited Quetzalcoatl to commit sins of drunkenness, vanity, and incest. Quetzalcoatl fled Tollan in shame and spent the remainder of his life as a penitent, wandering from kingdom to kingdom, until he reestablished his cult at Cholula. His days ended on the coast of Veracruz, where he either died or, as legend tells, sailed over the horizon on a raft of serpents promising to return one day to reclaim his kingdom of Tollan (**Plate II**).[6] The "Children of Quetzalcoatl," noble families who promoted the cult of the exiled hero, dominated southern Mexico for more than two centuries prior to the rise of the Aztec Empire.

Following the collapse of Tollan sometime around AD 1200, the Mexica moved south to Lake Texcoco. Impoverished and subjected to attack by local warlords, they retreated to an island where they witnessed a miraculous vision, again foretold by their god Huitzilopochtli: an eagle standing on a cactus growing from solid bedrock, the sign for their final destination of Tenochtitlan. As mercenary warriors feared by rival Toltec factions, the Mexica gained political and economic power, achieving control of central and southern Mexico, and eventually bestowing their name on an entire nation. Officially founded in 1325, the city of Tenochtitlan (today's Mexico City) rose to its height as the imperial capital (**Plate III**).[7]

More than a century passed before the Mexica attained full hegemony. Through a series of strategic alliances marked by factionalism and treachery worthy of the Roman Republic's period of civil conflict, the Mexica succeeded in expanding their domain to the south and east along the lake, eventually forming the Aztec Empire of the Triple Alliance with the neighboring city-states of Texcoco and Tlacopan.[8] For the remainder of the fifteenth century, Motecuhzoma I and his successors Axayacatl and Tizoc charted the course of Aztec expansionism (**Plate IV**). Tizoc's brother Ahuitzotl was appointed *huey tlatoani* (emperor) in 1486. An able military commander, he reorganized the army and initiated long-distance campaigns on an unprecedented scale. Under Ahuitzotl, the empire reached its apogee, dominating as many as twenty-five million people living throughout the Mexican highlands.

Ahuitzotl died in 1502 and was succeeded by his nephew, the ninth *tlatoani* Motecuhzoma II Xocoyotzin (familiarly known as Montezuma or Moctezuma), the ruler who suffered the Spanish invasion under Hernan Cortés in 1519 (**Plate V**).[9] Faced with internal dissent and the impossibility of raising an army from among the few Mexica communities that remained loyal, Motecuhzoma II was ill-equipped to confront the Spanish soldiers and the multitudes of native confederates. He opted for a diplomatic solution, with fatal results. Failing in every attempt to hold the conquistadors at bay, he invited Hernán Cortés into Tenochtitlan, only to be taken hostage. According to an eye-witness account of the conquistador Bernal Díaz del Castillo, Motecuhzoma died after he tried to quell a popular uprising and was pelted with stones. Native sources, however, indicate that he was executed by a Spanish soldier when the revolt of Tenochtitlan's people rendered him worthless to his captors.[10] His successor, Cuitlahuac, succumbed to smallpox, a disease that decimated millions and vanquished the Aztec empire more surely than any invading army. Motecuhzoma's nephew, the nobleman Cuauhtemoc (Falling Eagle), was elected *huey tlatoani* and directed the final heroic defense of the metropolis until its fall on August 13, 1521. Fleeing the destruction of Tenochtitlan, Cuauhtemoc was seized on Lake Texcoco, tortured by a deputy of Cortés in a vain quest for the coveted Aztec gold, and finally executed in 1525.

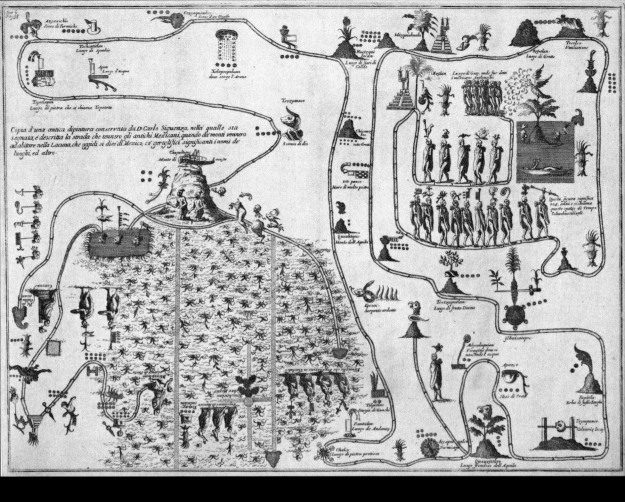

I | **Aztec Pilgrimage Map** | Andrea Magliar (Italian, active 1690s) | Engraving in Giovanni Francesco Gemelli Careri, *Giro del mondo* (Tour of the World), Naples, 1700, vol. 6, plate at page 38 | H 29.5 × W 40.5 cm (11⅛ × 16 in.) | Research Library, the Getty Research Institute | 2698–167

Gemelli Careri embarked on a world tour in 1693, reaching Mexico in 1697 and residing there for a year. He based this engraving on a sixteenth-century map, known as the Mapa Sigüenza, which tells the story of the wanderings of the Mexica from their mythic origins in Aztlan to their homeland in Tenochtitlan. The events shown here took place over the course of a century; the map thus represents a journey through time and place. Beginning in the upper right corner, footprints mark the tribe's route, with hill glyphs representing the cities in which the Mexica stopped along the way to the Valley of Mexico near Chapultepec (Hill of the Grasshopper). The site of Tenochtitlan is denoted by a nopal cactus at the lower end of Lake Texcoco.

II | Quetzalcoatl, from Apaxco | About 1500 | Basalt | H 70 × W 49 × D 44 cm (27½ × 19¼ × 17⅜ in.) | Museo Arqueológico de Apaxco, Instituto Mexiquense de Cultura | I–10832

Occasionally Aztec sculptors carved images of Quetzalcoatl with the face of the hero emerging from the jaws of a serpent to suggest that the man could become the creature and the creature could become the man. Valuable feathers from the quetzal bird cover the serpent's coils. The earliest representations of this kind date to Mexico's Preclassic period (1500–200 BC) and also appear on Olmec monuments, demonstrating the antiquity of combining the attributes of a tropical bird, a serpent, and a human. As a god, Quetzalcoatl was responsible for creating the people of the world and was credited with discovering maize. As a man, he was considered to be the founder and high priest of the city of Tollan (Tula), until forced into exile by his nemesis Tezcatlipoca.

The publication of Hernán Cortés's second and third letters to Charles V included a map of Tenochtitlan (present-day Mexico City), the earliest plan of a city in the Americas. Reputedly based on the conquistador's sketch, the map depicts topographical details of the Aztec capital that were not documented in Cortés's report and are likely indebted to an indigenous prototype. The Templo Mayor and *tzompantli* (skull rack) are accurately situated in a square ceremonial precinct within a circular island-city, echoing Aztec conceptions of Tenochtitlan as the center of the cosmic order. Despite the European-style residential districts shown in perspective—a feature owed to the Nuremberg engraver—the towering twin pyramids and emphasis on the city of Culhuacan, which prominently juts into the lake, are more faithful to native traditions. At the upper left, a flag bearing the two-headed eagle of the Hapsburg crown marks the site of Coyoacan, Cortés's base following the defeat of Tenochtitlan.

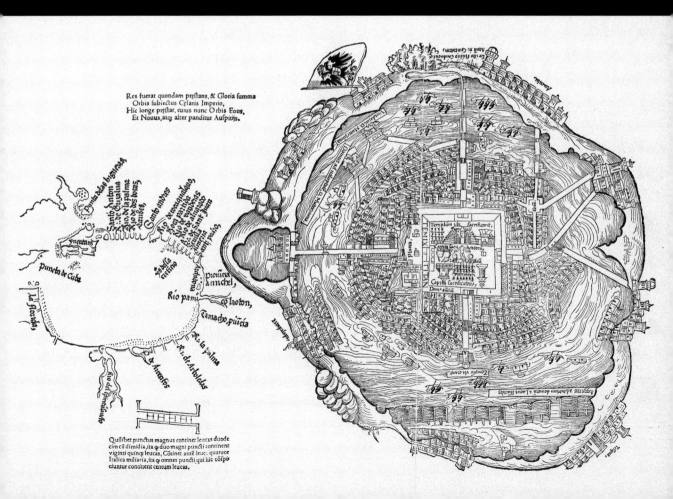

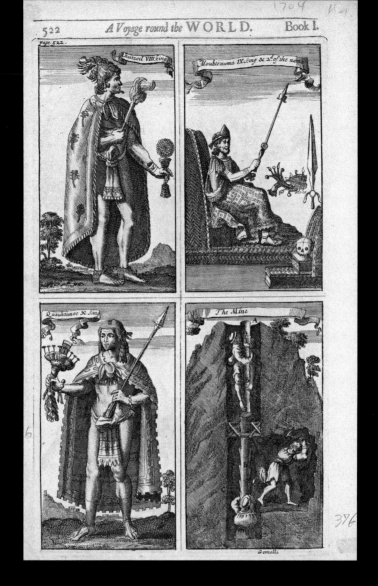

IV | **Aztec Rulers** | Andrea Magliar (Italian, active ca. 1690s) | Engraving from Giovanni Francesco Gemelli Careri, *A Voyage Round the World*, London, 1745, page 522 | H 32.2 × W 20.9 cm (12⅝ × 8¼ in.) | Research Library, the Getty Research Institute | P840001*

As the pre-Hispanic world faded from memory, illustrations created during the early Colonial period were continually reprinted. Portraits of the Mexica emperors Ahuitzotl, Motecuhzoma, and Cuauhtemoc were based on the Codex Ixtlilxochitl now preserved in the Bibliothèque Nationale in Paris. Each of the lords wears an ornate cape (*tilmatli*) and a *maxtlatl*, a loin cloth tied at the front. Motecuhzoma occupies a throne constructed of a woven grass mat, a traditional symbol of royal power. Careri's schematic image of local mining techniques alludes to Mexico's abundance of precious ores and minerals, which were exploited in the colonial era.

TO
RITR. DI MOTEZVMA
LE
CAVATO DALL ORIGINA:
MO
VENVTO DAL MESSICO
AL SER: G.D. DI TOSCA: NA

Suor Isabella P.F

V | **Motecuhzoma II** | Isabella Piccini (Italian engraver, 1644–1734), after Antonio Rodriguez (Mexican, 1636–1691) | Engraving in Antonio de Solís, *Istoria della conquista del Messico* (History of the Conquest of Mexico), Venice, 1704, plate at page 246 | H 19 × W 14 cm (7½ × 5½ in.) | Research Library, the Getty Research Institute | 93–B9622

Engraved after a late seventeenth-century portrait of Motecuhzoma II in the Museo degli Argenti in Florence, this image captures the noble bearing of the Mexica monarch. Eyewitnesses described him as dark skinned, of medium height, and slender build with a large head, an aquiline nose with flat nostrils, wavy hair, and a thin beard. He dons a romanticized version of the typical garb worn by Aztec rulers. The gold bands adorning Motecuhzoma's arms and legs, his *maxtlatl* or loincloth, and the heavy cloak reflect ethnographic images in sixteenth-century codices, but have been embellished with numerous fanciful European details. As a young man, Motecuhzoma II had proven himself a devout priest with a predilection for sorcery, as well as a capable military leader, who sponsored lucrative military campaigns in Oaxaca, Guerrero, Veracruz, and coastal Chiapas. His vassals both feared and respected him, which made his accommodating response to the Spanish threat puzzling. A number of factors doubtless inhibited his ability to engage the Spaniards militarily, ranging from internal factionalism among his nobles to the fact that the Aztecs only waged war during a specified time of the year in coordination with the agricultural cycle.

FIGURE 2 | **Emblem of Charles V** | Luigi Marliano (Italian, before 1484–1521) | Engraving in Girolamo Ruscelli,
Le imprese illustri … (The Illustrious Emblems …), Venice, 1566, plate at page 111 | H 17.3 × W 12.7 cm (6⅞ × 5 in.) |
Research Library, the Getty Research Institute | 87–B3573

The classical lens through which conquistadors and missionaries regarded the peoples of the New World was rooted in the recovery of the Graeco-Roman heritage in Spain during the Golden Age. At the court of Charles V, antiquity was a potent marker of imperial authority. Following his 1477 marriage to Mary of Burgundy, the Holy Roman emperor Maximilian I engaged Europe's foremost humanists to construct a pedigree that would legitimize his claims on much of Europe, and even on the papacy itself, by tracing the family's ancestry back to Charlemagne, the Roman emperors Augustus and Julius Caesar, and ultimately to the legendary Trojan hero Aeneas. Through the unification of the

Conquistadors, Missionary Orders, and the Classical Heritage

Austro-Burgundian and Spanish royal houses, Maximilian bequeathed to his grandson—Charles, who became king of Spain in 1516—not only material wealth and power on an unprecedented scale, but also an extraordinary legacy of mythic entitlement. Spectacle and the visual arts were essential devices in furthering Charles V's aspirations for a universal monarchy. Less than a decade after sacking Rome, the king staged a classical-style triumph there that the victorious Roman general Sulla would have envied. A bronze portrait statue of the monarch subduing Fury quotes an episode from Virgil's *Aeneid*. Clad in removable Roman armor, the body of the emperor is revealed beneath as a nude classical hero.[11] A cameo portrait by Leone Leoni pairs a profile of Charles, an avid collector of ancient gems, with that of his son Phillip II and a winged thunderbolt of Jupiter, presenting the monarchs as the true heirs of the Roman imperial rule.[12] Royal collections of ancient gems and statuary reflected the court's growing attachment to classical imagery, aesthetics, and ideals.[13]

The election of King Charles V of Spain as Holy Roman Emperor in 1519 was an event that united no fewer than four of the highest-ranking royal households in Europe. To signal his bid for a universal empire, Charles commissioned a heraldic device that featured the Pillars of Hercules, the gateway to the Atlantic. According to Greek myth, Hercules, the legendary founder of Spain, raised the mountains at the straits of Gibraltar as "pillars" to mark the farthest boundaries of the known world. On them was inscribed the motto *Ne Plus Ultra*: beyond which nothing. Adopting *Plus Ultra* (more beyond) as his personal motto, Charles redefined the pillars as a portal to the expansive Habsburg sovereignty, which now extended from Europe to the Americas and Asia and encompassed conquered territories never imagined by the ancients. Symbolic of the king's outward-looking ambitions, a banner bearing the *Plus Ultra* motto interlaces the columns of the imperial emblem (**Figure 2**). Charles V's inversion of the classical myth to transcend the achievement of the greatest ancient Greek hero was part of his court's broader adaptation of classical iconography, but his emblem held far greater implications for the future course of empire.[14]

The tradition of *ars historica* as humanist study was shifting away from the fabrication of royal pedigrees to the determination of new forms of political thought, law, and government.[15] The discovery of the New World brought with it the revelation of a people who had no fixed place in written history and whose existence was not foretold in the Bible. Who were the Aztecs and where did they come from? What laws were to be applied to them? Cortés's letters to the Spanish court described Tenochtitlan's temples, ceremonial plazas, and palaces, prompting comparisons to what his Spanish audiences did recognize—the fabled cities of Troy, Jerusalem, Carthage, and Rome. Perceived as a civilization that existed outside the condition of salvation, the Aztecs were framed as historical equivalents to the ancient Romans prior to the advent of Christianity.[16] If the Aztecs inhabited an antique world, then seemingly they should be governed by the laws of antiquity. Classical history and philosophy were drafted to define the relationship between Spain and its New World subjects, a matter of some urgency in the face of the unanticipated sophistication and complexity of Amerindian society.

Nowhere were classical sources more pertinent than in the conquistadors' assertion of the Roman legal principle of *de jure belli,* or right of conquest by just war. The philosophical basis for *de jure belli* was promulgated by the Dominican friar Francisco de Vitoria (about 1485–1546), a professor of theology at the University of Salamanca.[17] Vitoria has been dubbed the "father of international law" for his strikingly modern advocacy of the essential rights of the indigenous peoples of New Spain. Although condemning the atrocities of the conquistadors—and, by the same token, the rites of Aztec human sacrifice—Vitoria marshaled the model of Roman imperialism and based his analysis on the alliance that Cortés had established with several disaffected indigenous city-states. By 1519, the Children of Quetzalcoatl (the confederacy of nobles that dominated southern Mexico) had been subjected to seventy-five years of nearly continuous warfare with the Empire of the Triple Alliance. Surrounded and cut off from allies and from their sacred pilgrimage center of Cholula, the Tlaxcalteca faction of the confederacy complained to Cortés that they had suffered so many privations in their efforts to withstand the Mexica that they lacked such basic commodities as salt.[18] On the basis of the ancient Roman principle *causa sociorum et amicorum* (for the sake of allies and friends), Vitoria argued that Cortés's was a just conquest:

> This is how they say the Tlaxcalteca (Talcathedani) acted against the Mexicans. They made an agreement with the Spaniards that the latter help them and possess whatever might come their way by the law of war. For the fact that aid to allies and friends is a just cause of war is not in doubt … and this is confirmed by the fact that it was indeed especially by this method that Romans expanded their empire … and by undertaking just wars upon this opportunity they came by right of war into possession of new provinces. And yet the Roman Empire is approved as lawful by Saint Augustine … and by St. Thomas.[19]

Spanish-Amerindian relations reached a crucial turning point during the "Controversy of the Indies," a debate that took place in Valladolid in 1550–1551 at the order of Charles V. A referendum on the morality of imperial power, the debate pitted Juan Ginés de Sepúlveda against Bartolomé de las Casas, a Dominican bishop of Chiapas and fierce defender of Indian rights.[20] Both adversaries turned to the heritage of Greece and Rome to denigrate or elevate natives under Spain's jurisdiction. Sepúlveda cited Aristotle's concept of natural slavery to argue for the justice of Spanish subjugation of "barbarian" nations. Las Casas praised Aztec accomplishments over those of the Romans and daringly ventured the point that human sacrifice was not unknown in European history. He drew parallels between contemporary Spaniards and their pre-Roman Iberian forebears. Indigenous Iberians had suffered oppression as vassals of the Roman Empire, Las Casas argued, in equal measure to the cruel injustices visited upon Nahua natives in the name of the Habsburg monarch. As an early experiment in cultural relativism, the arguments put forward by Las Casas exposed the moral dilemmas of empire. Just as significantly, however, Roman narratives and counternarratives spurred Spanish humanists to engage in a critical analysis of ancient history and religion, while propounding a pioneering discourse on modern national identity. Experiences among the surprisingly sophisticated civilizations of the New World had the additional effect of encouraging humanists to investigate Europe's own antique past with fresh vigor.

The artifice of classical legality that supported the military objectives of the conquistadors was mirrored in the Christian evangelical missions of mendicant orders. Following the 1492 defeat of Granada, the last Islamic kingdom in Europe, Pope Alexander VI granted extraordinary privileges to the Spanish kings, appointing them heads of the Roman Catholic Church in their domains and thereby making the church an arm of the state. Priests had accompanied Cortés during the course of his military campaigns in the West Indies, but it was only in 1523 that the first missionary expedition of Franciscan friars arrived in New Spain. The Franciscans envisioned a realm where together with indigenous communities they would lay the foundations of a new Christianity. Missionaries strove to interpose themselves between conquerors and conquered by introducing the philosophy of their order while still preserving, at least in principle, the ideals of the native Mexica culture.[21]

No single historical resource has proven more valuable for comprehending Aztec civilization than the extensive reports compiled by a Franciscan friar whom many regard as a sixteenth-century pioneer of the field of anthropology. Fray Bernardino de Sahagún was born in 1499 in Sahagún de Campos, León, Spain.[22] Arriving in New Spain in 1529, he resided for the subsequent sixty years in and around the Valley of Mexico, teaching and writing in the communities of Tlatelolco, Tepepulco, Cholula, and Huextozinco. Disappointed with the superficiality of mass baptisms, he understood that the true conversion of the Aztec soul could only be achieved by learning everything possible about indigenous life, language, and systems of belief.[23]

Proselytizing was a two-pronged effort, which entailed instructing promising Aztec recruits in Christian doctrine and briefing church officials on native ritual practices, with the aim of devising the most effective pedagogical methods (**Figure 3, Plate VI**). Recognizing that there would never be enough priests to evangelize New Spain, Bishop Juan de Zumárraga directed the Franciscans to establish the Colegio de Santa Cruz in 1536 at Tlatelolco, a former city-state that had shared power with Tenochtitlan until it was defeated and absorbed into the metropolis. The Colegio was

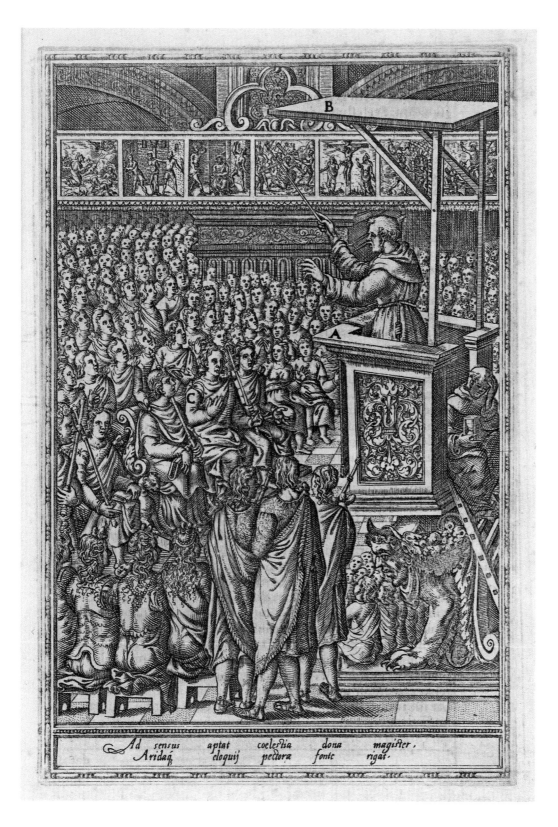

FIGURE 3 | **Friar Pedro de Gant Instructing Aztec Congregants** | Diego Valadés (Mexican, about 1533–after 1582) | Engraving in Diego Valadés, *Rhetorica christiana* ... (Christian Rhetoric ...), Perugia, 1579, plate at page 210 | H 19 × W 13.2 cm (7½ × 5¼ in.) | Research Library, the Getty Research Institute | 1388–209

the first university of the Americas. There Sahagún taught Latin, rhetoric, philosophy, and theology to the youths of the indigenous nobility to prepare them for the priesthood. He was officially commissioned by the head of his order to undertake a systematic investigation of Aztec ritual in 1558. Enlisting the most accomplished of his students as collaborators, Sahagún assembled a group of Aztec nobles from the community of Tepepulco and interviewed them for two years. Native informants supplied pictorial illustrations, for which Sahagún's student collaborators wrote explanations in the Nahuatl language. Known as the *Primeros Memoriales*, the manuscript is divided into four parts, describing the "Gods and Rites," "Heavens and Underworld," "Rulership," and "Things Relative to Man." Depictions of the dances and feasts performed in the central ceremonial precincts are particularly vivid, as is Sahagún's recitation of the gods' radiant ritual dress:

> The Array of Huitzilopochtli
> On his head is a headdress of yellow parrot feathers with a quetzal feather crest. His blood bird is on his forehead. There are stripes on his face, on his countenance. Ear plugs of lovely cotinga feathers. On his back he bears his fire-serpent disguise, his *anecuyotl*. On his arm is an armlet with a spray of quetzal feathers. The knotted turquoise cloth is bound around his loins. His legs are painted with blue stripes. On his legs are small bells, pear-shaped bells. His lordly sandals. His shield is the *tehuehuelli* [destroyer of people]. Across the shield lie stripped arrows. His serpent staff is in his other hand.[24]

Most remarkable is the evocation of ritual garb in such graphic, poetic detail, when a recounting of religious stories, or the natural domains over which the gods presided, would rather have been expected.[25] One has the distinct impression that by invoking articles of adornment, the spiritual power of the deity is called forth.

For Christian evangelists like Sahagún, the gods of the Aztecs were incarnations of the devil—but what kind? Like Cortés, Sahagún had been schooled at the University of Salamanca, a center of classical scholarship where Graeco-Roman polytheism was the familiar model of pagan cult. By the time Sahagún had revised the Aztec deity list for the first volume of his *Historia general de las cosas de Nueva España* (1575–1577)—a work commonly referred to as the Florentine Codex—these strange beings had become deceptively familiar. Organized as a pantheon, the gods were paired into couples, and various attributes were assigned to increasingly individualized characters so that they uncannily resembled anthropomorphic figures analogous to the gods of Greece and Rome (**Plate VII**).[26] For the edification of Spanish readers, the opening pages of the Florentine Codex explicitly identify the main Aztec deities with their Roman counterparts: "Vitzilobuchtli otro hercules, Tezcatlipuca otro iupiter, Chicomecoatl es otra Diosa ceres, Chalchiutliycue es otra iuno, Tlaçulteutl es otra venus, Xiuhtecutli es otro vulcan, Tezcatzoncatl, el dios del vino otro bacco."

In the third book of the Florentine Codex, Sahagún and his collaborators narrated the sagas of Huitzilopochtli and Quetzalcoatl in terms that betray other debts

17

to classical literature. Sahagún asserted that the Aztecs surpassed the Greeks and Romans in material achievements, political and social organization, as well as in the arts and sciences. Drawing parallels between incidents in Mexica and Graeco-Roman history, he compared the destruction of Tula to the fall of Troy as related in Virgil's *Aeneid*.[27] In the aftermath of the Trojan War, Aeneas wandered the Mediterranean before heeding a prophecy to go to Italy where his descendants would found a new nation: Rome. For Sahagún, the flight of Quetzalcoatl from Tula paralleled the legend of Aeneas. Just as the descendants of Aeneas had founded the eternal city, so the descendants of Quetzalcoatl had established Cholula, the largest pilgrimage and mercantile center in pre-Hispanic North America. Elsewhere in the Codex, the Aztec deity Chalchiuhtlicue is linked with Juno as a rain goddess having the power to make storms and sink ships (**Plate VIII**). Such a characterization of Juno has no equivalent in classical literature except in the *Aeneid*, when she provokes Aeolus to stir up a tempest against the Trojan fleet.[28]

The extent to which classical sources were available and read in New Spain can be measured through the book trade. At the Colegio de Santa Cruz, Sahagún's students were taught to regard Latin as the evangelical instrument of the Catholic Church and thus came to share their tutors' regard for ancient Rome as the touchstone of humanistic learning. The first library at Tlatelolco boasted sixty-one volumes, mainly consisting of ecclesiastical tracts. Students also had access to a number of secular books, including works by Cicero, Plutarch, and perhaps Appian's history of the Roman conquest of Spain.[29] Despite the efforts of church censors to limit reading material to appropriately pious topics, classical literature and medieval romances were regularly imported to New Spain.

Outside the college curriculum, the most popular book in early colonial Mexico was Andrea Alciati's *Emblematum Liber* (Book of Emblems), a compendium of moralizing proverbs paired with engravings, many illustrating stories from classical mythology. Combining verses and allegorical images, this immensely influential work must also have resonated powerfully with native traditions of pictorial manuscripts and poetry (**Plate IX**). Exposure to works from the classical canon as well as to popular encyclopedias of Greek mythology encouraged the sons of the indigenous elite to apply a classicizing gloss on Aztec history in the course of documenting their cultural heritage, as a first step toward empowering themselves in the emerging social order of viceregal Mexico. Bicultural and accomplished enough to teach Latin to incoming priests, Sahagún's outstanding students were handpicked to assist in the project of ethnographic documentation. With Latin as the lingua franca, a dialogue was established between Renaissance humanism and Aztec modes of thought, and the Valley of Mexico flourished—at least for a time—as a center of research on the life-ways and religion of the Aztecs.[30]

A telling example of the classical filter that Nahua scholars applied to Aztec history comes down to us in one of the most famous incidents of the Conquest (**Figure 4**). At the outset of his march on the Mexica capital in 1519, Hernán Cortés had participated in a remarkable Aztec ritual. According to native historians who described the event, Motecuhzoma II sent ambassadors to meet Cortés and present

FIGURE 4 | **Cortés Receiving the Aztec Ambassadors** | Watercolors in Bernardino de Sahagún, *Historia general de las cosas de Nueva España* (General History of the Things of New Spain), 1575–1577, vol. 3, fol. 415r–416r | H 24.1 × W 8.9 cm (9½ × 3½ in.) | Biblioteca Medicea Laurenziana, Florence | Med. Palat. 220

him with the raiment of four gods as a gesture of respect. When they reached the Gulf Coast of Tabasco, the ambassadors boarded the Spanish ship, knelt and kissed the deck in a gesture of reverence, declaring: "May it please the god to hear. His deputy governor Motecuhzoma, who rules Mexico for him, prays to him and says, 'The god has traveled far; he is tired.'"[31] Cortés was then dressed in the raiment of Quetzalcoatl, with a mask of turquoise mosaic over his face, a fan of quetzal feathers on his head, a tunic draped over his shoulders, and gold and jade necklaces circling his neck. Three other sets of ritual attire pertaining to Tezcatlipoca, the storm god Tlaloc, and the incarnation of the wind god Ehecatl-Quetzalcoatl, were laid out on the ship's deck before the Spanish commander. As illustrated in Book 12 of the Florentine Codex, Cortés then had the ambassadors chained to the deck and directed his men to demonstrate the firing of a siege gun. Terrified by the frightful display of superior technology, the ambassadors were given food and drink and sent back to Tenochtitlan to report to the emperor on all that they had seen.

Conventional readings of this incident hold that the superstitious Motecuhzoma II believed Cortés to be the priest-god Quetzalcoatl returned from the east. Yet other interpretations of this scenario are more likely. Calculated according to the Aztec calendar, the year 1519 corresponded to 1 Reed, a date regarded as sacred to the god Quetzalcoatl. Legends of returning gods were one means by which indigenous factions asserted political agendas, legitimized demands for changes in social order, or proclaimed open rebellion. A declaration of Quetzalcoatl's imminent arrival, therefore, may have been perceived as a genuine threat to the Aztecs, whose gods Huitzilopochtli and Tezcatlipoca had exiled this deity five hundred years earlier. Alternatively, the Aztecs were known to offer ritual dress to foreign dignitaries against whom they intended to wage war. Misunderstandings of the poetic style of Nahuatl oratory may have given rise to what some scholars now view as a revisionist myth—that the conquistadors were seen as divine—in order to explain the fall of Motecuhzoma's empire to a small band of soldiers. The honorifics paid to Cortés, in fact, were intended to convey just the opposite—the superior authority of the Aztec ruler.[32]

The story of Quetzalcoatl's reappearance and the gullibility of the Aztec emperor, not to mention a number of literary flourishes in which this legend is couched, derive mainly from post-Conquest histories. They raise questions about the motivation to depict the Aztecs as naive and timorous—all other accounts being to the contrary—and the inevitability of Cortés's victory. Comets, starbursts, spontaneous combustion, monstrous births, and other omens foretelling doom occur in identical form in three Latin texts: *The Jewish War* by Josephus, Lucan's *The Civil War*, and Plutarch's *Life of Caesar*.[33] Most likely contributed by Latinate Nahua authors, these interpolations have cast doubt on the authenticity of the Quetzalcoatl episode, but more significantly, they reveal conscious borrowings from classical legends to ennoble a unique chronicle of native religious belief.

A former student of the classics at the University of Salamanca, Cortés would have grasped the symbolism of donning the god's raiment, particularly given the penchant of ambitious Spanish and Italian nobles of the time to identify themselves with Graeco-Roman gods and heroes. Cortés never wrote of the incident and doubtless with good reasons, not the least of which was that he had just allowed himself to be revered as the incarnation of a pagan idol. Nevertheless the ritualized performance that Cortés and the Mexica ambassadors enacted poses several provocative questions. How did imperial rulers on both sides of the Atlantic wield myth-history as a stratagem to strengthen political power with a solid foundation in tradition? To what extent did reenacting deities serve as propaganda to underscore direct links between rulers and ancestral cult figures? How did a classical past legitimate and reinforce the ideologies of imperial elites?

VI | Aztec Sacrifice and Scenes of Daily Life | Diego Valadés (Mexican, about 1533–after 1582) | Engraving in Diego Valadés, *Rhetorica christiana*… (Christian Rhetoric…), Perugia, 1579, plate at page 172 | H 31 × W 21.6 cm (12¼ × 8½ in.) | Research Library, the Getty Research Institute | 1388–209

As the ruins of the Great Temple and other structures disappeared from memory, sixteenth-century writers and artists devised imagery of Tenochtitlan from fragmentary memories. In part a portrayal of the ritual practices carried out in the central ceremonial precinct, Valadés's bird's-eye view positions the Templo Mayor at the center of Mexica daily life. Surrounding the temple, the residents of Tenochtitlan navigate the lake on a balsa raft, fish, and prepare tortillas. These activities transpire in a grove of exotic Mexican plants, including *maguey* (agave), *flor* (maize), *cacao*, and an *arbor santo* (sacred tree) dripping water from its leaves.

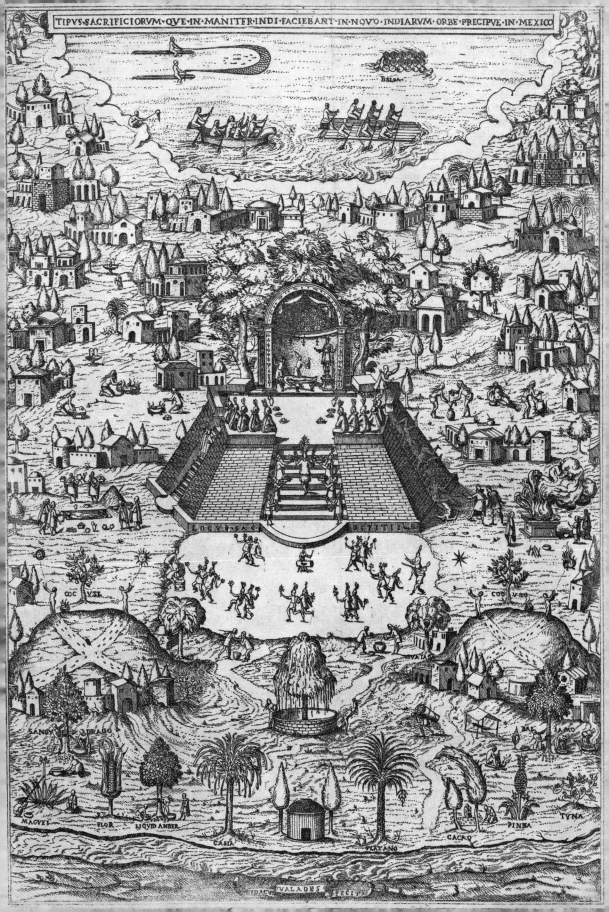

TIPVS·SACRIFICIORVM·QVE·IN·MANITER·INDI·FACIEBANT·IN·NOVO·INDIARVM·ORBE·PRECIPVE·IN·MEXICO

BALSA

COCCVSI

COCVLSO

SANGVIS·DRAGO

MAGVEI · FLOR · LIQVID·AMBER

CASA

PLATANO

CACAO

PINNA

BALSAMO

TVNA

DIDACVS·VALADES·FECIT

Quetzalcoatl.

Capitulo quinto. fo ibidem.

Chicome coatl. es otra diosa c̄

Capitulo septimo.   fo. 3.

Cioacoatl.

Capitulo sexto,   fo ibidem.

Teteu inna.

Capitulo octauo. fo. 16

Tzapotla tena.

Capitulo noueno.   fo. 4.

Chalchiuhtli   yeue, es otra iu

Capitulo onze   no, fo. 5.

Cioapipilti.   Ninfas.

pitulo deamo,   fo, ibidem

Tlaçulteutl. es   otra Venus.

Capitulo dozeno,   fo, 6.

(previous page) **VII | Aztec Deities |** Watercolors in Bernardino de Sahagún, *Historia general de las cosas de Nueva España* (General History of the Things of New Spain), 1575–1577, vol. 1, fol. 10v–11r | approx. H 31 × W 42 cm (12¼ × 16½ in.) | Biblioteca Medicea Laurenziana, Florence | Med. Palat. 218

Friar Bernardino de Sahagún is widely regarded as a pioneer of ethnographic technique, in which native informants draw pictures in order to recreate social memories of ancient rituals. Sahagún's project to document Aztec culture in Spanish and Nahuatl was controversial from the outset, yet he succeeded in assembling an incomparable account of native religion, culture, and history. After the Council of the Indies and the Holy Office (Inquisition) banned all works written in indigenous languages, the friar's magnum opus was sent to Spain and later to Florence. Copies of the *Historia* circulated after his death in 1590, but the original text (now familiarly known as the Florentine Codex) only came to the attention of scholars in the nineteenth century.

(right) **VIII | Noblewoman or Goddess**, from the Valley of Mexico | About 1500 | Diorite | H 80 × W 37.5 × D 27.5 cm (31½ × 14¾ × 10⅞ in.) | Museo Nacional de Antropología, Mexico City | 10–82215

There is little question that with the emphasis on militarism in Mexica society, women had to adopt specialized strategies to exert their rank and social authority. Whether this figure represents a noble woman or the goddess Chalchiuhtlicue is unclear, as she lacks identifying attributes, but the sculptor has lavished attention on her fine dress and intricate coiffure. She appears to be a young woman of marriageable age, who wears a cape called a *quechquemitl* over a skirt embroidered with an intricate design. Europeans remarked that palace women were accomplished weavers and embroiderers, and that a lord with many wives could count himself well off for the highly prized garments that they produced. Women were primary sources of wealth, enriching the palace and bringing prestige to the royal family. Their marriages formulated the web of alliances that bound city-states into powerful confederacies.

ΓΑΝΝΥΣΘΑΙΜΗΔΕΣΙ

GANYMEDES

Alciati's book of 212 emblems, each comprised of a proverb, picture, and a Latin epigram, was the most popular book in Mexico in the sixteenth and seventeenth centuries. Accompanying an illustration of Jupiter carrying off the beautiful youth Ganymede, the verse below advises that "It is the man who finds satisfaction in the counsel, wisdom and joys of God who is thought to be caught up into the presence of mighty Jove." Classical myths were frequently given a Christian gloss, but the illustrations and accompanying didactic messages also address practical and political concerns. This volume was dedicated to the Spanish monarch Charles V's envoy to Venice, Don Diego Hurtado de Mendoza, a poet, diplomat, and celebrated collector of art and Greek manuscripts.

Lorenzo Pignoria augmented Cartari's popular manual on the Graeco-Roman pantheon with illustrations of Mexican and Japanese gods in an appendix titled *Seconda parte delle imagini de gli dei indiani*. His illustrations were modeled on the Codex Vaticanus A, a colonial Mexican pictorial manuscript that describes Aztec religion and sacred ritual in unparalleled detail. Pignoria's identification of Homoyoca as a deity confused the name for the highest of thirteen heavens (Homeyocan, or Place of Duality) with the god who presided there, Ometeotl (Lord of Duality).Wearing a feathered headdress, Ometeotl sits on a litter of maize and holds a spray of quetzal feathers. Alleging that Mexican gods were related to the gods of ancient Egypt, Pignoria compared the pose and dress of codex images with Osiris from the Tabula Isiaca, an Egyptian-style bronze relief that was discovered in Rome in 1527. In the Renaissance, widely-read histories of mythology gave rise to spurious links between ancient and foreign polytheism, perpetuating the imposition of Old World paradigms on the complex cosmology of the Aztecs.

Beginning with the culture hero Huitzilopochtli, who is likened to the divinized hero Hercules, Bernardino de Sahagún paralleled Mexican and ancient Mediterranean gods according to basic complementarities between their domains and powers. Polytheistic religions presuppose an array of divine beings that hold sway over the human and natural spheres. It is therefore not surprising that divine will is connected almost universally with fruitful crops, success in war, favorable weather, and other aspects of the human condition. Adapted from the Greek notion of a pantheon of Olympian deities, the Romans conceived of a governing hierarchy of gods who wielded the

Parallel Pantheons

greatest influence over human affairs and the cosmos. Rituals were dedicated to a host of deities, introduced from the early religious traditions of archaic Italic peoples and from Magna Graecia, and later amalgamated with imported foreign mystery cults. Worship was formalized in the ceremonies of household and civic religion. Originally centering on *numina*, or spiritual and ancestral powers, religion was organized around a crowded calendar of festivals, the sacred space of sanctuaries and temples, and the performance of complex rituals, such as sacrifice and augury, administered by a professional priesthood. Myths of the gods' familial relationships and their interventions in mortal concerns were primarily a literary phenomenon, much of it borrowed from the Greeks, but the Romans also had their own tradition of myth-historical legends about their foundation as a people, codified in Virgil's *Aeneid*, the national epic.

This much of a basic picture of ancient Roman religion was available to Europeans like Sahagún, who were university educated in Spain's leading centers of classical humanism. Secular literature in the form of Latin historical texts furnished a working model of pagan beliefs that could be applied to peoples slated for conversion to Christianity. Europeans were heir to an intellectual tradition that encouraged comparisons between pagan religions, which were often understood as allegories. In addition to the idealized Olympian deities of classical mythology, sixteenth-century mythographers were intrigued by the bizarre, the foreign, and the mysterious features of Graeco-Roman cult. Seen through this lens, the image of the Aztec gods was warped, a treatment that was extended to pagan gods in general, resulting in numerous strange, pseudo-antique images (**Plates X, XI**).

When Renaissance antiquarians began to scrutinize ancient sculptures and coins, they saw reflections of the gods in essentially human form. The appearance in European art of classical deities as dignified beings sharing mortal concerns opened a wide gulf between the gods of Greece and Rome on the one hand and those of contemporary "heathen" cultures on the other. Sahagun's Nahua students endeavored to close this gap by presenting their cultural heritage in terms that were comprehensible to European eyes, while at the same time seeking status in the new social order. In cataloguing the full spectrum of Aztec life, including cosmology and divination, the friar had a different objective: that of the conversion and ultimate salvation of native souls. Despite its evangelizing purpose, the Florentine Codex provides a wealth of ethnographic information, which suggests several functional analogies between the ancient Mediterranean and fifteenth-century Mexico: what roles did ritual play in the statecraft of these two cultures, and how did religious pageantry further the goals of empire?

Since the Conquest, the nature of the Aztec gods has been a source of considerable scholarly debate. Based on surviving pre-Hispanic pictorial manuscripts, illustrated studies created after the fall of Tenochtitlan, and archaeological evidence of stone and clay cult images, it seems that most deities were conceived anthropomorphically. Some also manifested themselves through animal counterparts called *nahuals*, as for example Quetzalcoatl, who is represented as an enormous plumed serpent (**Figure 5**). Generally invisible, the gods could appear in dreams and visions, especially when invoked through the use of hallucinogenic plants and other stimulants. Deities were described as residing in a multilayered series of celestial and subterranean worlds. The storm god Tlaloc (**Figure 6**), the sun god Tonatiuh, and the death god Mictlantecuhtli (**Plate XII**) were believed to preside over specific domains where the souls of the deceased traveled. Directional characteristics were associated with these realms of the dead: Tlalocan was thought to lie to the east for example, while Mictlan was located to the north. Post-Conquest accounts occasionally allude to kinship among the gods, who may be husband and wife or parent and

FIGURE 5 | **Plumed Serpent** | About 1500 | Basalt | H 22 × W 45 cm (8⅝ × 17¾ in.) | Museo Nacional de Antropología, Mexico City | 10–220930

child, but the sources describe so many variant relationships that any rigid concept of a family structure to define a hierarchy of gods is notably lacking.[34]

A fundamental tenet of the Aztec belief system was the conceptualization of deities in dual, quadruple, or even quintuple form. Dualities were especially important in a consort system that logically paired Tlaloc the storm god with Chalchiuhtlicue the water goddess, or Xochipilli (Flower Prince) and Xochiquetzal (Flower Quetzal), the god and goddess of royal feasts, marriages, and the arts.[35] When familial connections were left unclear, gender-based equivalencies were still operative. The goddess Chicomecoatl and the god Centeotl, for instance, were both regarded as patrons of maize cultivation (**Plate XIII**). A quadruple pattern was inspired by the fundamental ritual significance of the cardinal directions as a symbol of balance in the natural and social environment, a concept that was pervasive throughout the Americas. The deity was conceived in one of four guises—five with the inclusion of the center, the sacred direction—and each was differentiated by a sacred color.

Aztec cult finds certain parallelisms with the organization of Roman provincial religious cults in the role of tutelary deities, local tribal figures who were promoted in status by being incorporated with older and more established gods of city-states.

FIGURE 6 | **Reclining Figure of Tlaloc** | 1450–1521 | Basalt | H 74 × W 108 × D 45 cm (29⅛ × 42½ × 17¾ in.) | Museo Nacional de Antropología, Mexico City | 10–10941

earlier sources. Holding laurel branches, a Greek symbol of victory, the god is presented with a goat-like lower body that—absent the wings—recalls the Arcadian woodland god Pan of classical myth. Worshippers lay offerings before a pedestal on which weapons have been mounted in the style of a Roman trophy, and the god's shrine takes the form of a neoclassical colonnaded hall.

Somewhat more impartial were the illustrations produced in the Netherlands by the renowned printmaker Bernard Picart. As a Huguenot, Picart knew the fury of religious persecution in his native France. His collaboration with the publisher Jean Frederic Bernard resulted in an encyclopedic study of world faiths, *Cérémonies et coutumes religieuses de tous les peuples du monde*, which promoted an Enlightenment spirit of cosmopolitan tolerance.[44] Featuring more than two hundred and fifty illustrations of religious customs throughout the world, Picart drew on a wide variety of written and pictorial sources for inspiration, irrespective of their inherent cultural preconceptions. In the sole depiction of human sacrifice included in Picart's description of pre-Hispanic ritual, the Great Temple is shown as a modest wooden post construction ornamented with human skulls, above which are two hut-like shrines (**Plate XIX**). The structure is miniscule by comparison with the actual Great Temple of Tenochtitlan, which loomed above a cult precinct of towering pyramids and expansive plazas. Seated on an orb within a shrine, a cult statue of Huitzilopochtli holds four spears and a shield of feathers. Little else of the god's dress bears any resemblance to earlier written or pictorial descriptions belonging to Mexica traditions.

On a following plate, Huitzilopochtli's image evinces an incongruous fusion of classical and Aztec iconography, evident as well in the depictions of the gods Tezcatlipoca and Tlaloc who are portrayed in the poses of enthroned Olympian gods. Cult figures on pedestals, housed in an open-sided domed shrine and approached by gesticulating worshippers, probably drew inspiration from engravings of the classical pantheon, for instance Hendrik Goltzius's engraving of Jupiter seated on a throne beside his eagle.[45] Within the chapel, Huitzilopochtli's image is placed before a rich drapery in a lavish shrine, presiding from atop an orb on a tall pedestal ornamented with weapons like a Roman trophy. Here Picart was more faithful to historical accounts in adding a sculpted hummingbird (more dove-like in appearance) to the god's headdress. No less regal in appearance, Tezcatlipoca sits on a Roman-style camp chair like a conquering general, albeit with a contorted, ape-like face (**Plate XX**). In a scene of worshippers before a seated figure of Quetzalcoatl, a feast dedicated to the god at Cholula is under way. Identified here as the Mercury of the Mexicans, Quetzalcoatl occupies a neoclassical pedestal in a tiled plaza surrounded by a European balustrade, which locates the setting at the top of a pyramid. His association with the Roman Mercury, god of trade, is doubtless a reference to Cholula as a major center of commerce (**Plate XXI**).[46]

Conflating geographical distance with a chronological gap of many centuries, gods from far away inhabited the same conceptual plane as those from long ago, in a process that detached Aztec religious practices from their cultural specificity. During the 1990s, postcolonial theorists argued that such images confirmed the impracticability of even attempting to understand the ancient art of the Aztecs, much less the ritual ideology behind it, especially given the fact that its original creators had long vanished. Even the very questions that one must pose as a scholar—such as whether the Aztecs conceived of their deities as a pantheon—betray a biased European world view and mode of inquiry.[47] Alternative approaches try to account for such distorted images by examining underlying principles of complementarity between Aztec culture and the colonial interpretations applied to it.[48]

As early as in the first century AD, Pliny the Younger had described many of the attributes of the monstrous races of humanity, which Christians later applied to Satan.[49] By the sixteenth century, a highly developed mythology of European characters had evolved, many of which were blended with the attributes of witches and devils as Christian theologians sought to define the positive or negative in the supernatural. The attributes of these creatures, in turn, were projected onto the Aztec gods. An evolution of image and idea can be charted in which the iconographic traits of a European witch-like being named Wild Woman were intentionally superimposed on Cihuacoatl (Serpent Woman), the patroness of midwives and healers—unkempt hair, emaciated body, ravenous teeth, and claws—largely to discredit the indigenous skills of a particular category of medical practitioners under the tutelage of the goddess.[50] In reality, these community health professionals represented a lingering and still potent threat to the successful evangelization of the Aztec people more than a century after the great civic temple cults had been eliminated.

The stereotypical images of pagan religion as devil worship that were imposed on the Aztec gods were not entirely projections. There is no doubt that the Aztecs conceived of their gods as frightening creatures. Large cadaverous effigies from the House of the Eagles, with skeletal heads and a liver protruding from the exposed ribcage, convey the terrifying aspects of the gods who governed the underworld (**Plate XXII**). Cihuacoatl—so frequently depicted with a fleshless human skull—was no exception, and in the colonial period she came to be seen as a co-ruler of Mictlan, which was equated with Hell. How did the Aztecs interpret and employ the formidable power latent in such images? Although no firsthand sources written by native theologians survive, both historical and contemporary studies of the continuity of Mesoamerican ritualism point to the capricious ambiguity in the gods' powers. In other words, what is feared or may cause death is simultaneously celebrated as a benevolent source of social well-being and bodily health. Such perceptions are confirmed by the verbal accounts of Sahagún's indigenous collaborators. For the capable Aztec midwife, Cihuacoatl was not so much to be feared as respected; she was addressed as Tonantzin, or "Our Mother." During labor Cihuacoatl could either take the life of a newborn child or grant it, but her power was not attributed to any innate disposition; rather, it was dependent upon the skills of her practitioners as well as on the performance of the correct rituals before and during labor.

Wild Woman could "make herself at home in colonial Mexico precisely because the Aztecs, however different from the Spaniards, expressed their values and concepts in metaphorical terms that were often remarkably congruent with those in Europe."[51] The complementarity in semiotic codes encouraged a reshaping of pre-Hispanic belief systems to conform to European conceptual templates, particularly during the later seventeenth and the eighteenth centuries, when the Inquisition overshadowed humanistic studies.

Buried under the zocalo for hundreds of years, demonized for evangelical purposes, or tamed with the civilized accoutrements of familiar classical deities, the Aztec gods were soon to reassume a conspicuous presence in Mexican culture. When the last great political and social reformer, Viceroy Juan Vicente de Güemes Padilla Horcasitas y Aguayo, 2nd Count of Revillagigedo, ordered the repaving of Mexico City's central plaza in 1790, workers made an astounding discovery: a colossal statue of Coatlicue, the decapitated mother goddess of Huitzilopochtli and therefore of the Mexica as a people (**Figure 7**).[52] One can only imagine the spectacle of workers digging the sculpture out day by day. With its massive claws for hands and feet, it must have appeared as if the goddess were literally crawling out of the very matrix of the earth. Consisting of three tons of rock and towering at a height of more than eight feet, Coatlicue is frightful to behold. Two massive spouts of blood surmounted by the undulating heads of snakes replace her face. A necklace of human hands, hearts, and a human skull pendant partly conceal her bare breasts. Wrapped around her waist is a garment woven of writhing rattlesnakes, which gives us her name: Serpent Skirt. On the eve of Mexican independence, the Aztec gods were returning to reclaim their rightful place as the symbols of a new nation of Mexico.

At the end of that same year a colossal disk of carved basalt, ten feet in diameter, was unearthed. The Calendar Stone—as it has come to be known—was probably conceived as a type of *cuauhxicalli*, a ritual receptacle intended for offerings of sacrificial human hearts and blood. A tour de force of concept and execution, the disk is carved with a series of complex symbols and intricate designs arranged in concentric circles around the face of a deity identified either as Tonatiuh, the sun god, Yohualtecuhtli, a personification of the sun in the underworld, or Tlaltecuhtli, the earth goddess.[53] Viceroy Revillagigedo was cognizant of the groundbreaking archaeological discoveries that had been made in Herculaneum and Pompeii, which were sponsored by the Bourbon king Charles VII and his son Ferdinand. The Mexican scientific community had long been following the excavations of the Vesuvian cities with keen attention and, in fact, the first Mexican publication of an archaeological nature was a 1748 report on the Roman ruins around the Bay of Naples.[54] The viceroy had the great Coatlicue monument removed to the Real y Pontificia Universidad de México for preservation, where it was temporarily displayed side by side with casts of Greek sculptures. Installed before the western tower of the cathedral, the Calendar Stone stood on public view in the center of the capital for more than a century.[55]

Monoliths continued to be uncovered throughout the remaining years of the eighteenth century. Many had been battered by hammering in a furious attempt to obliterate offending features, particularly the iconography associated with death and sacrifice (**Plate XXIII**). By the mid-nineteenth century, Mexican intellectuals and politicians were promoting Aztec heritage to underscore Mexico City's predominance as an ancient capital and to distinguish the country's cultural heritage from that of Spain. Recognizing the importance of antiquities as fundamental symbols of national identity, Cabinet minister Lucas Alamán enacted a decree issued by Congress that provided for the establishment of the first Mexican National Museum

FIGURE 7 | **Coatlicue**, found in Mexico City | About 1500 | Basalt | H 2.57 × W 1.30 m
(8 ft. 5⅛ in. × 4 ft. 3⅛ in.) | Museo Nacional de Antropología, Mexico City | 11-3329

in 1825, an event that closely coincided with Greece's independence and formation of an antiquities museum in Athens. By then, the great porphyry head of the
legendary moon goddess Coyolxauhqui had been excavated and placed on display
(**Plate XXIV**). With her serene yet noble countenance, this imposing relief quickly
joined the other icons of Mexica art. On her cheeks are hieroglyphic symbols for
golden bells—hence her name, "Bell Faced"—while nose and ear ornaments are
testament to the exalted position she held as a Toltec *tecuhtli*, or noble ruler. Shortly
thereafter, the Temple Stone was recovered from the site of what is believed to have
been Motecuhzoma's palace. Possibly serving as a throne for the last pre-Hispanic
emperor, the backrest portrays an image of Motecuhzoma II together with the god
Huitzilopochtli dedicating a *cuauhxicalli* as a symbol of a new era of Mexica rule.
Remarkably, the backside of the stone depicts the first pre-Hispanic evidence for
what had just been adopted as the heraldic seal for the Mexican flag, a relief of the
eagle standing on the cactus that symbolized the founding of Tenochtitlan.[56]

Imagine di Serapi Dio delli Egittÿ inteſo da loro per il
Sole, & per il Nilo, co'l ſimulacro d'vn corpo con tre ca
pi ſignificãti li tre tempi paſſato, preſente, & auenire,
& il Sole andar con ordine & miſura ne mai deuiare.

XII | Goblet with Mictlantecuhtli, from the Templo Mayor | 1450–1521 | Alabaster | H 16.5 × W 12.4 × D 9.9 cm (6½ × 4⅞ × 3¾ in.) | Museo del Templo Mayor, Mexico City | 10–168816

Though the original purpose of similar goblet-like vessels is uncertain, this example contained cremated human remains and may have been carved specifically for burial. Mictlantecuhtli was the lord of the dead who resided in a desert-like underworld of permanent twilight. Souls strong enough to survive a series of challenges through nine realms were guaranteed a place of permanent rest in Mictlan.

XIII | Incense Burner with Chicomecoatl, from Tlahuac, Mexico City | 1325–1521 | Terracotta and pigment | H 105 × W 72 × D 48.5 cm (42 × 28¾ × 18¼ in.) | Museo Nacional de Antropología, Mexico City | 10–571544

Incense burners conveyed messages to the gods on the smoke of burning copal, an aromatic pine resin. Applied as mold-made elements, the attributes of the deity adorning the front of the censer indentify the spirit force to which prayers are to be directed. In the Florentine Codex, Chicomecoatl was compared by Sahagún and his Nahua collaborators with the Roman goddess Ceres (see Plate VII). Both were the focus of their society's principal agricultural cults, maize for the Aztecs and wheat for the Romans. Chicomecoatl's name is a calendrical date marking her birth and feast day of Seven Snake.

XIV | Tezcatlipoca | 1450–1521 | Basalt | H 12.1 × W 14.9 × D 6.7 cm (4¾ × 5⅞ × 2⅝ in.) | Museo Nacional de Antropología, Mexico City | 10–9682

According to legend, Tezcatlipoca was the archrival of Quetzalcoatl. He was largely responsible for the hero's exile and ultimately for the civil war that led to the destruction of Tollan. The Acolhua in particular claimed him as their tutelary god and maintained his image in a sacred bundle at Texcoco. This diminutive figurine may have been contained in such a bundle. Carved on top of the head is his calendrical name, One Death.

XV | Cache Offering #106, found in the Templo Mayor, Mexico City | 1325–1502 | Basalt, bone, terracotta flint, obsidian, and shell | H 40.6 × W 109.2 × D 96.5 cm (16 × 43 × 38 in.) | Museo del Templo Mayor, Mexico City | 10-252003

Excavations at the Templo Mayor (Great Temple) in Mexico City unearthed an array of human, animal, and plant remains together with objects made of gold jade, turquoise, obsidian, silver, crystal, copal incense, rubber, and coral. Dedica tions were carefully packed into masonry cache boxes, which were sponsored by the principal tributary states. Among the faunal remains are sea creatures intended to signify the expanse of the Aztec domain from ocean to ocean. Some caches contain the figure of a seated god who has been variously interpreted as a mountain deity named Tepeyolotl (Heart of the Mountain), or as a god who rep resented a paramount lord named Xiuhtecuhtli (Turquoise Lord). Many sculp tural objects are typical of the peoples conquered by the Mexica, particularly in southwestern Mexico. Offerings were made to commemorate rituals of social advancement, the funerals of dignitaries, and the construction of new building phases of the Great Temple.

XVI | Funerary Urn with Tezcatlipoca, found in the Templo Mayor, Mexico City | About 1450–1500 | Terracotta | H 32.9 × W 17.5 × D 9.5 cm (12¹⁵⁄₁₆ × 6⅞ × 3¾ in.) | Museo del Templo Mayor, Mexico City | 10–168823

When Aztec nobles died they were dressed in the guise of the deity they served and then were cremated. In this way the personality of the deceased was sublimated to that of the god. One of a pair, this funerary urn excavated at the Templo Mayor is stylistically associated with the earlier Toltec civilization, suggesting that the deceased wished to be connected with a more ancient tradition in death. The relief image is that of Tezcatlipoca (Smoking Mirror), who is identifiable by the image of a mirror that replaces his left foot. Regarded as the god of fate, Tezcatlipoca was the patron of kings, magicians, and necromancers, and was renowned for revealing the future by means of a polished obsidian mirror.

XVII | **Xochipilli**, found in Tlalmanalco, on the slopes of the volcano Popocatepetl | 1450–1521 | Basalt | H 117 × W 55.5 × D 45 cm (46⅛ × 21⅞ × 17¾ in.) | Museo Nacional de Antropología, Mexico City | 10–222160/2

Widely regarded as a masterpiece of the human form by any standards, this sculpture of the god of royal feasts, poetry, games, and dance is unusually animated, as if caught in the act of singing a chant. He wears a mask and his hands may have held musical instruments. Intricate reliefs adorn his body and the platform on which he sits, representing such potent hallucinogenic plants as psilocybin mushrooms, morning glory, and peyote. These substances not only induced intoxication but were believed to enable those who consumed them to see and speak with the gods and the spirits of deceased ancestors. Xochipilli, a name meaning simply Flower Prince, was the patron god of the royal palace and is recognizable by the distinctive flowers carved in relief across his body.

Viztliputzli idolum Mexicanorum.

XVIII | Huitzilopochtli Idol of the Mexicans | Engraving in Arnoldus Montanus, *De Nieuwe en onbekende weereld, of Beschryving van America en 't zuid-land* (The New and Unknown World, or Description of America and the Southland), Amsterdam, 1671, plate at page 220 **|** H 29 × W 34.8 cm (11⅜ × 13¾ in.) **|** Research Library, the Getty Research Institute **|** 93–B9309

Montanus, a Jesuit-trained Latin teacher, produced an atlas of the geography, natural history, and populations of North and South America. Like many illustrations of "heathen" civilizations, his depiction of native religious beliefs indiscriminately mixes features of different cultures with sheer fantasy. This widely circulated engraving reconfigures the Aztec god Huitzilopochtli as an incarnation of Satan, but the iconography also incorporates aspects of pagan deities from classical mythology.

XIX | Sacrifice of Captives | Bernard Picart (French, 1673–1733) | Engraving in Jean Frédéric Bernard, *Cérémonies et coutumes religieuses de tous les peuples du monde* (Ceremonies and Religious Customs of all the Peoples of the World), Amsterdam, 1723–1743, vol. 3, plate at pages 150–151 | H 15 × W 20.9 cm (6 × 8¼ in.) | Research Library, the Getty Research Institute | 1387–555

Two volumes of Bernard's encyclopedic investigation of world faiths are devoted to religious practices among "idolatrous peoples." This plate purports to depict rituals celebrated at Tenochtitlan's Great Temple. Twin vaulted edifices at the summit of the structure represent the temples of Tlaloc and Huitzilopochtli. The scene of human sacrifice, with a sacrificial victim tumbling down a narrow stair, is Picart's only depiction of the violent ritual, and was copied from José de Acosta's 1588 study of the New World.

Sacrifice des CAPTIFS.

VITZLIPUTSLI.

TLALOCH, ou TESCALIPUCA.

TESCALIPUCA representé d'une autre façon.

PRÊTRES MEXICAINS.

Le MERCURE des MEXICAINS adoré à CHOLULA sous le nom de QUETZALCOUATL.

XXI | The Mercury of the Mexicans Worshipped at Cholula Under the Name of Quetzalcoatl | Bernard Picart (French, 1673–1733) **|** Engraving in Jean Frederic Bernard, *Cérémonies et coutumes religieuses de tous les peuples du monde* (Ceremonies and Religious Customs of all the Peoples of the World), Amsterdam, 1723–1743, vol. 3, plate at page 156 **|** H 15 × W 21 cm (6 × 8¼ in.) **|** Research Library, the Getty Research Institute **|** 1387-555

Quetzalcoatl wears a rounded cap similar to that of Mercury, the Roman god of commerce. The Aztec priest-hero's odyssey from Tula to Cholula was celebrated by more than a dozen different ethnic groups throughout southern Mexico, who claimed that the penitent hero had traveled through their kingdoms to establish his cult. Cholula was a major market and pilgrimage center, and the principal source of religious and political cohesion. Quetzalcoatl's cult was maintained by a confederation of merchant-lords, who competed to sponsor an annual feast dedicated to the god, for which they gained titles to high office in the city's administration.

Goddesses like Cihuacoatl were associated with a broader category of Erinyes-like spirit beings called tzitzimime (sing. tzitzimitl), who wielded frightening powers. Tzitzimime personified an indigenous belief in the connection between disease, drought, war, sacrifice, death, and divine castigation. One of a male-female pair, this life-size representation of a tzitzimitl (often identified as Mictlantecuhtli, Lord of Death) was found in the House of the Eagles at Templo Mayor. Wearing a loincloth and sandals, the death god menacingly extends clawed hands. Traces of blood detected on its surface corroborate the practice of human sacrifice, although the scale of this ritual reported in sixteenth-century sources is certainly exaggerated. Most feared during climactic events such as eclipses, tzitzimime were believed to emerge as stars to attack the sun and bring an end to the present age of mankind. Issuing from clouds bringing rain, water, thunder, and lightning, the tzitzimime were associated with fertility as well as with the chaos induced by drunkenness and violent discord.

XXIII | Xiuhtecuhtli, found near the Templo Mayor, Mexico City | 1450–1521 | Basalt | H 80.6 × W 55.2 × D 42.5 cm (31¾ × 21¾ × 16¾ in.) | Museo del Templo Mayor, Mexico City | 10–650349

Recently excavated from the ruins of a *calmecac* (elite religious and military academy) in the ceremonial precinct of Templo Mayor, this figure represents the solar god Xiuhtecuhtli, whose name means both Fire Lord and Turquoise Lord. Xiuhtecuhtli was a patron god of kings, and midwives performed special bathing rituals for children in his honor. Despite the evidence of intentional damage, the shape of a royal crown is visible. Many Aztec sculptures have been destroyed beyond recognition, either at the hands of conquistadors or later by native Mexicans, who sought to annul any lingering spiritual energy. Distinctions between conqueror and conquered became ambiguous in the colonial period in Mexico, and the Indians who buried these figures may have been equal participants in deactivating them.

XXIV | Coyolxauhqui, found near the Templo Mayor, Mexico City | 1450–1521 | Green porphyry |
H 72.5 × W 85.5 × D 64.5 cm (28½ × 33⅝ × 25⅜ in.) | Museo Nacional de Antropología, Mexico City |
10-2209118

The Spaniards were not entirely misguided in their conception of Aztec society as a living manifestation of the ancient civilizations of the Mediterranean. After all, everywhere they looked they would have envisioned in the exuberant colors and textures of daily life what in their homeland could only be dimly gleaned from the writings of Roman historians and the remains of Roman Hispania. In the Middle Ages, church doctrine taught that the ancient world was primarily the stage for the birth of Christ and the spread of Christianity. The iconography of classical gods and heroes, however, permeated medieval art, architecture, literature, and astrology, safely disguised behind edifying allegories of Christian morality.[57] Vestiges of Greek and Roman cities were just as ubiquitous and it was the Renaissance achievement to cast the light of intellectual inquiry on their physical remains. It is no coincidence that just as coins, inscriptions, and artifacts began to be valued as independent witnesses of the past, Spanish antiquarians were developing a new regard for the customs of contemporary non-Europeans. The idea that different civilizations pass through similar stages of progress justified the comparison between present-day Aztecs and ancient Romans. The encounter with Amerindians thus sparked new interest in antiquities, particularly on the Iberian Peninsula.

Art and Empire: From Roman Hispania to New Spain

Many of the conquistadors were natives of Extremadura, a western Spanish province that was formerly part of Roman Lusitania. Imperial cities such as Itálica, the birthplace of Trajan, and the capital of Mérida (Emerita Augusta) preserved substantial examples of Roman-era architecture, notably theaters, amphitheaters, temples, and private villas.[58] Drawings by the Flemish topographical artist Anton van den Wyngaerde were commissioned by Ferdinand II to document leading cities and ruins, and constituted a groundbreaking visual survey of the historical landscape in the mid-sixteenth century (**Figure 8**).[59] Emulating the Habsburg court and Italian aristocrats, Spanish nobles competed to collect Roman statuary to adorn their palaces and gardens.[60]

Though the artisanry of Aztec gold and featherwork excited the admiration of European artists and found a place in cabinets of curiosities, there is no evidence that large-scale sculptures were appreciated as aesthetic objects in the way that Graeco-Roman statuary was. Unique among pre-Columbian sculptural traditions, Aztec artists were exceptionally skilled in portraying human and animal forms. Some Aztec sculptures, in fact, later inspired direct comparison to works of the classical period. The nude female figure found in Texcoco is a characteristic example of Aztec freestanding sculpture created in the imperial style. Her realistic, subtly modeled flesh and musculature combined with abstract facial features would not have been unfamiliar to Archaic Greek or Etruscan sensibilities (**Plate XXV**).[61] The custom of invigorating statuary with bright painted colors and added eyes of shell or white stone was also shared, although the degree to which these attributes endowed classical sculpture with same sense of life force as they did for Aztec objects is open to debate.[62]

Zoomorphic *cuauhxicallis*, such as the monolithic eagle from Templo Mayor charged with delivering human hearts—the sacred food of the gods—would scarcely look out of place in ancient Rome. Its plumage delineates the curve of the bird's powerful neck and breast, accentuating the eagle eye and hooked beak (**Plate XXVI**). Analogous sculpted figures of eagles occupied a singular place in the arts of the ancient Mediterranean, as symbols of divine authority and bearers of omens, and in Rome they were the standard visual insignia of Jupiter, the emperor, and of the cult of the army. Motifs with an eagle rending a serpent recur in European and non-Western art, a seeming transmission that has long intrigued art historians.[63] Rather than seek out aesthetic similarities and differences, however, we may consider the Aztec *cuauhxicalli* and the Roman eagle as useful metaphors for how public art and monumental constructions created a communal identity and a cultural "commons" in a heterogeneous empire (**Plate XXVII**).

Derived from the Latin term *imperium*—legally sanctioned power and the lands controlled by that power—the very notion of empire has its roots in the ancient Mediterranean. An empire is a state established by conquest, which claims sovereignty over extensive territories and incorporates a sizeable populace within a centralized administrative system.[64] Supported through tribute or direct taxation, imperial administrations must deploy a sizeable military force to defend frontiers. Although empires impose hardships on subject peoples, they can also offer advantages: protection from external aggression, maintenance of law and order, and enhanced production and prosperity. Imperial economies encourage and sustain dense populations—particularly within capital cities—which can be used to raise armies or to supply colonists required for territorial expansion. The inhabitants of a capital city are divided into economic classes with a broad distinction between elites and commoners.

Because the local states, chiefdoms, and tribes that come under the sway of an imperial regime can vary widely in terms of languages, cultures, and religions, empires are characteristically cultural mosaics.[65] Incorporating the multicultural agendas of

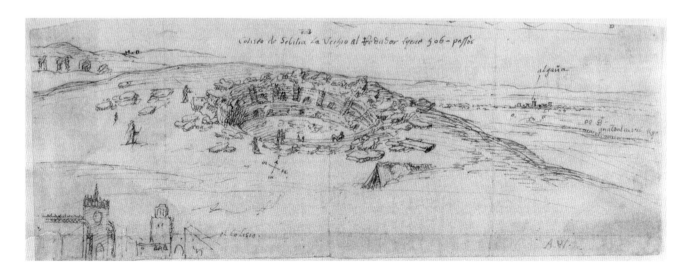

FIGURE 8 | **Amphitheater at Itálica** | 1567 | Anton van den Wyngaerde (Flemish, 1525–1571) | Pen and brown ink | H 10.4 × W 29.8 cm (4⅛ × 11¾ in.) | Victoria and Albert Museum, London | inv 8455, 15ro

the conquered and their social, ritual, and linguistic differences into a cohesive political entity entails formidable challenges. Empires are unwieldy in scale and difficult to govern solely through military might; as a result, a number of strategies evolve, which can be conceived as indirect or "soft" imperialism. Though warfare and tribute were at the heart of Aztec imperial control, these mechanisms could only be effective on a long-term basis when materialized in the form of architectural monuments, warrior costumes, and the ideologies that stood behind their creation and use.[66] All the cunning and skill of architects and artists were enlisted to perpetuate the illusion and reality of dominance, as well as to create a sense of shared history and identity. Life-sized figures such as that of the Eagle Warrior, for example, manifest the martial virtues that were at the center of the Mexica's imperatives of perpetual warfare, conquest, and sacrifice (**Plate XXVIII**). Few societies, ancient or modern, staged the ideologies of a theocratic state in such visually compelling terms.

Ancient Rome perfected the art of symbolic display by means of a series of magnificent imperial building programs and public installations of honorific statuary. With the defeat of Carthage—its chief Mediterranean rival—in 146 BC, Rome engaged in military expeditions throughout Greece and Asia Minor. In the Hellenistic kingdoms of Pergamon and Alexandria, conquering generals marveled at monumentalized cityscapes. They commissioned similarly imposing building projects back in Rome, in an effort to redistribute their extraordinary gains and build coalitions among the capital's political factions. During the late Roman Republic, Gnaeus Pompeius Magnus (later known as Pompey Magnus, or Pompey the Great) stands out for his savvy exploitation of the public's inherent appetite for spectacle as entertainment.[67] Although the ways in which wealth might be redistributed to gain power were restricted, effective avenues were available to politically ambitious citizens. On his return from campaigning in the eastern Mediterranean, Pompey produced a triumph that lasted two days. Winding through the city for miles, a procession of wagons and portable tables reenacted dramatic highlights from key battles, showcased captive monarchs, and displayed the loot from fourteen nations and nine hundred cities that the general claimed to have defeated. By means of such elaborate spectacles, he succeeded in overshadowing his predecessors, eclipsing his rivals, and equating himself with Alexander the Great in the eyes of the Roman people. How could he insure that such power might last?

Pompey had encountered architectural wonders in the great theaters of the eastern Mediterranean and recognized what powerful social tools they could be. Despite the prohibitions against permanent theaters in Rome on the basis of moral, political, and security grounds, he invoked the right of the triumphant to dedicate religious edifices. Pompey undertook the construction of a massive new theater, the cavea of which was effectively a staircase leading up to a temple of Venus Victrix (Venus the Conqueress). The largest public building of its day, the structure was dedicated as a temple and positioned Pompey in a state of permanent triumph. The sheer scale of the theater—reputed to seat an audience of 40,000—guaranteed his ability to affect the political current to his benefit by regularly sponsoring lavish entertainments. Roman citizens were the direct beneficiaries of the autocrat's largesse and were thereby induced to embrace his authority in practice, if not in sentiment. On the threshold of empire, the cult of personality had become a critical strategy.

Modern historians refer to the deployment of architectural and artistic monuments for political purposes in terms of a "theater-state," where spectacle communicated the emperor's might and values in a potent exercise in statecraft.

Augustus, Rome's first emperor, transformed the sponsorship of monumental edifices and public art into a political institution that spread across the Mediterranean and Europe. Completing Caesar's building programs and renovating the old Roman Forum, he erected a temple consecrated to his illustrious great-uncle, the deified Julius, which he dedicated in 29 BC. Construction of the new Forum Augustum was coupled with the erection of a temple dedicated to Mars the Avenger, fulfilling Augustus's boast of having transformed a city of brick into one of gleaming white marble.[68] A number of Greek features are reflected in the design of the Forum Augustum, not the least of which was an elaborate decorative program of more than a hundred bronze and marble sculptures, forming the backdrop for military ceremonies and religious rituals. At the center was a portrait statue of the emperor mounted in a triumphal chariot. In the apse of the Temple of Mars Ultor stood a statue of the war god, flanked by figures of Venus, ancestress of the Roman people, and the deified Julius Caesar. Portrait statues of great generals who had been awarded triumphs, prominent civic leaders, and heroes were displayed along with images commemorating the Julian-Claudian line back to the mythic progenitors Romulus and Aeneas. Aptly labeled the first "hall of fame," the Forum was a monumental labor of visual propaganda, where the legacy of Augustus's achievements was permanently enshrined together with that of his forebears—a dramatic celebration of the divine lineage that empowered his imperial successors.[69]

On the eve of its destruction, Tenochtitlan rivaled and in many ways surpassed the Rome of the Caesars. Hernán Cortés and his soldiers were likely not cognizant of Roman architecture and public sculpture as powerful political weapons in the service of the theater-state. Although some of his men had served in Italy in the previous decade during Spain's wars against the French, their imagination of classical antiquity was fired instead by the sagas of Alexander the Great, Hannibal, and Julius Caesar, whose conquests of vast territories and fantastic races of humankind were inspirational models to them. Rome's urban grid plan, roads, and grand central plazas were later exports to New Spain, but it is easy to envisage how the splendor of Tenochtitlan could have summoned immediate comparisons with antiquity's greatest metropolises. Conquistadors were the first Europeans in more than a millennium to witness an apparently ancient empire come to life before their very eyes. They observed firsthand the efficacy of religious spectacles as a validation of a theocracy with expansionist aims, and expressed their admiration through the filter of Amadis of Gaul, a popular romance from the *reconquista* of the Moors: "…when we saw so many cities and villages built in the water and other great towns on dry land and that straight and level causeway going towards Mexico, we were amazed and said that it was like the enchantments they tell of in the legend of Amadis, on account of the great towers and cues and buildings rising from the water, and all built of masonry. And some of our soldiers even asked whether the things that we saw were not a dream."[70]

Tenochtitlan and neighboring Tlatelolco boasted a population of more than 200,000. Together with the million or more residents of adjacent communities around the shores of Lake Texcoco, many of which were joined to the city by cause-ways, the Valley of Mexico hosted one of the largest urban complexes in the world. Wealth flowing into the capital from scores of tributary city-states allowed the Mexica to undertake the construction of massive public works. Miles of aqueducts brought fresh water into the city, protective dykes crossed Lake Texcoco, and an extensive system of *chinampas* (raised fields) multiplied the agricultural productivity of the island. Spectacular temples built of masonry, finished in dazzling white plaster and frescoed in polychrome hues of red, blue, and yellow, were surrounded by well-ordered neighborhoods and markets stocked with products from throughout the realm.

By 1500, the Mexica had developed a complex social organization, fusing elements of the preceding Toltec city-state and Chichimec tribal organizations to realize a new imperial order. The *huey tlatoani* was an elected position with preference given to royal brothers and nephews. A system of checks and balances on the *huey tlatoani*'s authority was overseen by a priesthood supervised by the *cihua-coatl,* who headed the war council and governed the city when the emperor commanded the army in the field. The upper classes were composed of nobles—*pipiltin* (sing. *pipil*)—and lords—*tetecuhtin* (sing. *tecuhtli*)—many of whom resided on estates worked by peasants or slaves (**Figure 9**). Tenochtitlan was organized into residential districts, or *calpulli,* whose members, the *macehualtin,* claimed affiliation through kinship groups. Each *calpulli* owned lands communally, elected civic leaders, worshipped its own gods, and fought together as a military unit.

Members of the ruling class devoted a considerable part of their lives to public worship and ceremonies. Their presence was called for on every occasion to coordinate, supervise, and perform in the festivals. This role assured that constituents perceived them as the source from which all benefits of membership in Mexica society flowed. Four of the festivals were designated as the time during which tribute—the lifeblood of the city—was paid by conquered provinces and redistributed to the populace. Every year during the festival of Huey Tecuilhuitl (Great Feast of the Lords) the *huey tlatoani* supplied the entire population of *macehualtin,* the peasant class that composed the majority of Tenochtitlan's citizenry, with food and drink for seven continuous days. Aztec festivals not only conveyed the image of divine blessing but also reinforced the established hierarchies of the social order.

No fewer than eighteen principal feasts were celebrated every twenty days throughout the year, most of which were dedicated to the promotion of agricultural fertility. In addition, a system of moveable feasts was coordinated with the principal market days and timed to the 260-day divinatory calendar. Festivals were characterized by such opulent displays of pageantry that the city must have existed in a state of perpetual celebration. These events, in fact, were carefully coordinated so that every conceivable segment of society—nobles, soldiers, young men, girls, dignitaries, merchants, weavers, jewelers, feather workers, or huntsmen—was celebrated throughout the year. All festivals were characterized by parades, dances, music, singing, poetic recitations, speeches, theatrical performances, and ritual combats, as well as extremely bloody rituals of human sacrifice.

In February, the annual cycle began with rites dedicated to the storm god Tlaloc and the flayed god Xipe Totec (**Plate XXIX**). During the festival of Tlacaxipehualiztli,

FIGURE 9 | **Nobleman or standard-bearer**, found in Churubusco, Mexico City | About 1500 | Basalt |
H 80 × W 32 × D 18 cm (31½ × 12⅝ × 7⅛ in.) | Museo Nacional de Antropología, Mexico City | 10–81575

captive nobles equipped with simple wooden swords were forced to defend themselves in hand-to-hand combat against a host of well-armed warriors. Once defeated, they were sacrificed and the skin was cut from their bodies. After it was dried, specially designated priests would trim, lace, and wear the flayed skin. Masquerading as the god Xipe Totec, the priests would then beg for alms for the sick.[71] In the belief that masking and ritual dress facilitated access to the divine, deity impersonation was a fundamental characteristic of nearly every ritual performance. During the festival of Toxcatl, for example, a youth was designated to impersonate the god Tezcatlipoca. Throughout the year he was treated as a living incarnation of the divinity until the appointed time of his ritual sacrifice (**Plate XXX**). At other times the nobles impersonated the gods. Tenochtitlan's high priest and commander-in-chief of the armed forces was given the title of *cihuacoatl* and attended ceremonial functions dressed as Serpent Woman, the mother-goddess.

The political and religious center of the Empire of the Triple Alliance was located within a great ceremonial precinct composed of more than seventy-five individual structures. According to legend, the Mexica constructed the Templo Mayor, or Great Temple, at the location on the island where the first tribal leaders witnessed an eagle perched on a nopal cactus, and placed a sacred bundle containing the image

FIGURE 10 | **Huitzilopochtli** | About 1500 | Jadeite | H 6.7 × W 4.1 × D 4.7 cm (2⅝ × 1⅝ × 1⅞ in.) | Musée du Quai Branly, Paris | M.H.30.100.43

of Huitzilopochtli within it (**Figure 10**). As their fortunes grew through military conquest, the Templo Mayor was expanded at least seven different times to demonstrate to the people that their labors were indeed fulfilling the destiny promised to them by their god.[72] Early illustrations indicate that the Great Temple platform rose in four stages and was surmounted by a pair of temples: one on the north side dedicated to the storm-god Tlaloc and another to the south belonging to Huitzilopochtli. The Mexica thereby married the principal cult of the more ancient Toltecs extending back to Tula and Teotihuacan, with that of the Chichimec tutelary deity, whose people had entered the Valley of Mexico more recently.

Numerous major works of Mexica sculpture found in and around the Plaza de la Constitución in the center of Mexico City are closely connected to the ritual activities conducted in the Templo Mayor, the remains of which were unearthed to the east of what is today the National Cathedral. Aztec architectural sculpture must not be considered simply as isolated pieces of statuary, but rather as profoundly symbolic elements of an ensemble, designed to create a physical context and mythic meaning for dramatic stories enacted by ritual impersonators.[73] Nowhere is this narrative more graphically portrayed than in the sculptural decoration of the Templo Mayor, which constituted an architectural realization of the Aztecs' founding creation myth of Coatlicue (**Figure 11**).[74] As told in the Florentine Codex, when Coatlicue was impregnated, her daughter Coyolxauhqui and four hundred sons plotted to kill her. The child in her womb was Huitzilopochtli, who emerged to slay Coyolxauhqui:

> Then he had his array with him, his shield, his spears, and his blue spear thrower, and with diagonal stripes was his face painted … he was pasted with feathers at his forehead and his ears … and he had stripes in blue mineral earth on both his thighs and his upper arms. Then he pierced Coyolxauhqui, and then quickly struck off her head. It stopped there at the edge of Coatepec, and her body came falling below, it fell breaking into pieces; in various places her arms, her legs, her body each fell.[75]

Then Huitzilopochtli turned on the four hundred brothers:

> [H]e pursued, gave full attention to the brothers; he scattered them from the top of Coatepec … and he chased them all around. In vain they went crying out to him, yet in vain … Uitzilopochtli just set on all of them; he indeed destroyed them; he annihilated them; he exterminated them … And when he had had his pleasure, he took from them their goods, their adornment, the paper crowns. He took them as his own goods, as if taking the insignia to himself … And they placed their trust in Huitzilopochtli. And this veneration was taken from there, Coatepec, as was done in the days of yore.[76]

Written in the 1570s, Sahagún's is a folkloric narration of the story of Coatlicue, Coyolxauhqui, and Huitzilopochtli, but the myth's actual staging at the Templo Mayor a century earlier must have been positively riveting.

FIGURE 11 | **Huitzilopochtli Defeating Coyolxauhqui and her Brothers** | Watercolor in Bernardino de Sahagún, *Historia general de las cosas de Nueva España* (General History of the Things of New Spain), 1575–1577, vol. 1, fol. 204v | H 22.7 × W 8 cm (9 × 3⅛ in.) | Biblioteca Medicea Laurenziana, Florence | Med. Palat. 218

When archaeologists discovered the Coyolxauhqui monolith in 1978, they soon realized that it lay in situ at the foot of the staircase of building Stage IV and probably dated to the mid–1400s, around the time of the reign of Motecuhzoma I. The goddess is portrayed lying on her side and stripped of clothing, the public humiliation of the defeated. Her limbs and head have been torn from her body, with the gaping wounds rendered by scalloped rips to the flesh and protruding limb bones. Undulating serpents bind her arms and legs and monstrous masks adorn her elbows, knees, and sandals. She was clearly a goddess who was intended to be every bit as fearsome in death as in life (**Figure 12**). Expanding the excavation, project director Eduardo Matos Moctezuma and his team discovered the Coyolxauhqui monolith in situ at the bottom of the stairs directly below the Temple of Huitzilopochtli. Further exploration revealed the existence of two enormous serpent heads at the foot of the staircase balustrades. Juxtaposed at the base of the pyramid, these sculptures identify the pyramid as Coatepec (Serpent Mountain), the locus of cosmic creation. Completing this narrative of the Aztec origin myth is the relief of the defeated Coyolxauhqui, whose dismembered corpse lay at the bottom of the landing.

FIGURE 12 | **Relief Sculpture of Coyolxauhqui**, found at the Templo Mayor, Mexico City | 1430–1470 | Basalt | Diam. 3.30 m (10 ft. 9⅞ in.) | Museo del Templo Mayor, Mexico City | 10–252739

Coyolxauhqui's downfall and the ascendance of Huitzilopochtli were reenacted by Mexica warriors and captives seized during military campaigns. Each sacrificial victim who mounted the stairs of the Templo Mayor thereby became an actor in a dramatic production intended to "bring home the war" to the citizens who had committed sons to the army and supplied food and resources for military operations. As embodiments of Huitzilopochtli, Aztec warriors were ever prepared to protect their family, *calpulli,* and city.[77] Captives assumed the role of cosmic enemies. They were living proof of Huitzilopochtli's omnipotent power, which was manifested in the ability of his spiritual descendants—his mighty warriors—to repay his blessings, the very livelihood that the Aztec people enjoyed. Pulled onto his back over the surface of a sacrificial stone, the captive was held down by four priests while a fifth drove a knife into his chest and slit the arteries of the heart (**Plate XXXI**). Lifting the bloody mass into the air, the priest pronounced it to be the "precious eagle cactus fruit," a supreme offering to the sun god. The corpse was then cast down the temple staircase onto the monolith bearing the image of Coyolxauhqui's dismembered body.[78]

Warfare, sacrifice, and the promotion of agricultural fertility were inextricably linked in religious ideology. Aztec songs and stories described four great ages of the past, each destroyed by catastrophes wrought by vengeful gods. The fifth and present world only came into being through the self-sacrifice of a hero who was transformed into the sun. Without a gift from humankind to equal his own, however, the sun would refuse to move across the sky. Warfare was required to feed the sun his holy food (blood) and thereby perpetuate life on earth. No such term as "human sacrifice" was used by the Aztecs, who considered the act a sacred debt repaid to the gods.[79] For the warriors, participation in these rituals offered an opportunity to demonstrate their courage, gain financial rewards from the emperor, and announce their promotion in society. Executions also served as a grim object lesson for visiting foreign dignitaries lest they ever venture into war against the empire.

The charismatic role of the *huey tlatoani* in sponsoring military rituals was graphically depicted on the Stone of Tizoc, which was used to secure a noble captive during gladiatorial combats.[80] Relief scenes depict Tizoc taking captives from fifteen different kingdoms and wearing the hummingbird headdress of Huitzilopochtli—proof that the emperor presented himself as the incarnation of the Mexica patron god while sponsoring sacrificial rites. Religious rituals advertised the prowess of his army and the riches from conquered lands that the ruler distributed to his people.

The emperor's sponsorship of significant architectural and artistic projects also promoted the spread of an imperial style in tributary provinces. Ahuitzotl directed the construction of a temple on a promontory above Tepoztlan in an effort to incorporate the local cult of the *pulque* deity Tepoztecatl into the larger cycle of agricultural festivals celebrated in the capital of Tenochtitlan (**Plate XXXII**). In 1501, he had a circular cave-like temple carved from the solid rock of a mountain above Malinalco, a town to the southwest of Tenochtitlan that served as a Mexica ritual and administrative center. Uniquely, the temple is preserved virtually intact, complete with rock-cut figures of eagle and jaguar seats. Both temples exemplify how Tenochca architectural styles functioned as ideograms to integrate conquered territories into the realm of the military state.[81]

Working from the premise that the superimposition of metropolitan artistic styles on subjugated territories can play a key role in regional politics, archaeologists have investigated the development of an imperial-style temple complex at the site of Calixtlahuaca (Morelos).[82] Recent excavations indicate that although the community was divided into at least two distinct ethnic components, Mexica-style architecture and statuary were confined to a single district of the site. The evidence that only part of the community practiced Mexica-sponsored rituals suggests that the central imperial administration sought to affect local politics by supporting a specific political faction, on whom the metropolitan cult was conferred.

Freestanding sculptures like that of Ehecatl-Quetzalcoatl pose challenging questions of interpretation (**Plate XXXIII**). Were art forms and architectural styles created by Mexica artisans subsequently impressed upon conquered states by the rulers of Tenochtitlan, or were provincial artisans induced by the nobility of Calixtlahuaca to emulate the style current in the capital as a gesture of consent to imperial domination? Comparative archaeology can be applied to test the alternatives and underscores a key strategy of colonial and imperial power: the decisive influence on the affairs of regional polities by elites, who may opt for (or be co-opted by) the central state authority. "Top-down" models that gauge the influence of local leaders call for equal attention to the lower economic sectors of society, especially at the margins of an empire's territory.

Similarly, studies of how Celtiberian communities in Hispania responded to "romanization" stress the diversity of possible scenarios, and the resilience of indigenous cultures despite the outward appearance of Roman lifestyles.[83] Acknowledging that Hispania holds a key to understanding the administration of the empire, archaeologists focus attention on the reorganization of urban topography, the presence of Italic architectural types (houses, baths, and temples), and the changing nature of religious beliefs. Because they dictate ways of living and governing, towns are the most obvious signs of "Roman-ness." Great public edifices and Latin inscriptions tend to suggest that a progressive reorientation toward a Roman world view took place, but this evidence pertains mainly to the urban elite who were the prime catalysts of cultural change. Augusta Emerita (Mérida)—with its temple, theater, and a forum embellished with a sculpture program similar to that of the grand Forum of Augustus in Rome—is an example of the success of the imperial project. Looking at domestic contexts, cemeteries, and religious sanctuaries from outside the Roman *colonia*, however, can reveal much more of an interplay between Italic and Iberian systems. Here we find that cultural ambidexterity or "code-switching"—the selective adoption of certain traits and traditions as the social context calls for it—is a better index of identities in the fluid and ambiguous circumstances of empire.[84] Pre- and post-Conquest Mexico, where multicultural and multilingual communities came into close contact, invite an analogous approach.

The Holy Roman Emperor Charles V's passion for the trappings of classicism left a vivid imprint on the arts and culture of viceregal Mexico. Festival books illustrated his every triumphal entry into conquered cities, and this tradition found receptive audiences among the inhabitants of Mexico City. From the earliest days of the capital, ceremonial entries, masques, and dramatic performances were the main forms of public entertainment in Mexico City.[85] Theatrical productions traditionally facilitated the evangelizing process as priests resorted to plays in their duty to popularize Christianity. Cortés was hailed by throngs of the city's residents on his return from Honduras, where he endeavored to relieve the people from corrupt imperial officials. When Don Antonio de Mendoza made his entry as the first Viceroy of Mexico City in 1535, he was duly fêted as the emissary of the Crown's authority with celebrations that lasted for days. Triumphal arches were erected featuring paintings and sculptures that compared Mendoza with the classical gods and illustrated his divine pedigree.

Some festivals called for the erection of enormous sets, featuring forests inhabited by wild animals and birds, which were released and pursued by indigenous people to display their expertise in hunting. Díaz's written description calls to mind what the frescoes in the church of Ixmiquilpan—located to the north of the Valley of Mexico—vividly portray. Created in the mid-sixteenth century, the murals depict a forest in early Renaissance style with Aztec warriors hunting centaurs and doing battle with various other creatures from classical mythology. Jousts and bullfights were featured in the festivals, but most popular were mock combats, in which hundreds of masked and costumed performers played the roles of Greeks, Romans, Christians, Moors, Turks, and Aztecs.

In 1538, the city-state of Tlaxcala presented an elaborate spectacle of the siege of Jerusalem during the Feast of Corpus Christi, for which a garden, forest, villages, and castles were recreated.[86] All characters were played by the indigenous citizens of the community including prominent lords, many of whom no doubt had fought for the Spaniards during the conquest of Tenochtitlan. Tlaxcalteca organizers reconfigured the events of the siege, which occurred in AD 70, substituting Charles V for the Roman emperor Titus. Confronting an encamped army of Spaniards, the defenders were led by a "sultan" with an army of "Moslems and Jews," many of whom were actually Tlaxcalteca fitted out in their former glory as Indian warriors complete with weapons, feather shields, and headdresses. For all intents and purposes, the siege of Jerusalem was staged as an amalgam of episodes from the Conquest of Mexico and from contemporary conflicts with the Ottoman Empire. While there are no records of how pageants were produced, the conflation of historical events into highly charged vignettes became a primary tool of cultural integration. Government officials had become conscious of the tremendous diversity of the population to whom they needed to appeal. Whether addressed to Spaniards, mestizos, Creoles, or Indians, the festivals had to convey a visual message that was as politically integrative as possible while still reinforcing the primacy of the European social order.

Reenacting the Conquest was just as much an indigenous act of recording historical memory as it was for the Spanish. Drawing on eyewitness accounts that chronicled the events of 1519–1521, the Conquest of Mexico became a popular theme in colonial Spanish painting.[87] Most are formulaic in portraying such iconic events as the massacre of Cholula, the meeting of Motecuhzoma II and Cortés on the Tlalpan causeway, and the final siege of Tenochtitlan. In 1614, ornamental screens known as *biombos* were first introduced to the viceroyalty of New Spain from Japan through the Manila galleon trade. Treasured by the aristocratic families that commissioned them, ornamental room dividers usually depict panoramic historical, mythological, and religious subjects as well as scenes of festivities and quotidian activities.

Major episodes of the Conquest of Mexico transpire simultaneously across the ten folding panels of a screen in the collection of the Banco Nacional de México, as if on a vast stage (**Plate XXXIV**). Reading from right to left, the narrative begins and ends on the first panel, where Motecuhzoma II meets Cortés (top right), and the eleventh and last Aztec ruler Cuauhtemoc surrenders to Spanish soldiers (bottom right). Focusing on the events of November 1519 and the following eight months, the screen culminates with the *Noche Triste* (Night of Sorrows) on June 20, 1520, when hundreds of Spaniards and their native allies were slaughtered as they fled Tenochtitlan via the Tlacopan causeway. Commissioned primarily to commemorate a turning point in the foundation of New Spain, such screens actually represent highly interpretive reenactments of those events. The iconography is a creative visualization of contemporary conquest literature and may reflect ephemeral festival scenery as well. At the center, Motecuhzoma wears a European-style crown as he addresses his people. To his left, soldiers occupy the steps of the Great Temple at Tlatelolco, which resembles a flattened theatrical backdrop. Participants in the fighting seem to wear parade armor, a clear echo of Mexico City's frequent triumphal processions and pageants, when battles between the Spaniards and the Mexica were regularly reenacted. Heroic deeds are highlighted in equal measure, reflecting a proud acknowledgment of both the European and the indigenous past.

Having suffered the consequences of the Conquest and the loss of the world as they knew it, New Spain's indigenous people sought alternative paths to power through religious conversion. Many kingdoms formerly under the hegemony of the Aztec empire engaged the emerging political order peacefully, led by indigenous aristocrats (*caciques* or *gobernadores*), who assumed leadership positions in colonial society. Evangelization was given largely to the Franciscan and Dominican orders, which sent missionaries to all the ranking noble houses. Acting as mediators between the crown and the *caciques* who effectively controlled the land, the church succeeded in establishing enduring and lucrative partnerships. *Caciques* dressed as Spaniards, rode horses, and acquired titles to suit their elevated positions. They expanded their domains, built lavish palaces, and dedicated churches.

Making efforts to preserve their indigenous cultural traditions, New Spain's native elite were nonetheless drawn to the Christian pantheon of saints and hastened to assimilate them. Indigenous beliefs persisted in rural areas, where rituals were dedicated to the ever-present hope for fertility (**Plate XXXV**). Caves, sacred places in the natural environment, and in some cases sites that were formerly the locus of pre-Hispanic worship continue to be venerated throughout Mexico. Some still contain devotional objects associated with the ancient religious rites, even though today such sites are largely connected with the cult of the Virgin and other Christian saints. Mexico's patron saint, the Virgin of Guadalupe, is the most celebrated example of the cultural transformation of a native deity.

First published in the Nahuatl language by Luís Lazo de la Vega in 1648, the *Nican Mopuhua* (Here it is Written) tells the legend of Juan Diego Cuauhtlatoatzin, an indigenous resident of the Aztec city-state of Cuauhtitlan, who was among the first to be baptized by the Franciscans. In December 1531, Juan Diego had a vision of the Virgin Mary, who spoke to him in Nahuatl, indicating her wish that a shrine in her honor be built on the hill of Tepeyac. Juan Diego told the Bishop of Mexico, Fray Juan de Zumárraga, about this vision, but was dismissed since he could provide no proof. On his return to Tepeyac, the Virgin returned and commanded Juan Diego to gather the Castilian roses growing on the hillside. When the Bishop saw them he wept, for in addition to the miraculous sight of roses from his native Spain growing in midwinter, he beheld an image of the Virgin that had been impressed on Juan Diego's *tilmatli*, the cape in which he had carried the flowers. Today, the Catholic Church regards the Virgin of Guadalupe as the "Virgin Mother of the Americas."

Just as significant as the miracle is the place where it transpired. Tepeyac was the location of a pre-Hispanic temple dedicated to Tonantzin (Our Mother), an honorific given to Cihuacoatl and other Aztec goddesses. Though it had long since fallen into ruin, the site remained sacred to the indigenous community. In the Florentine Codex, Bernardino de Sahagún expressed dismay at the fact that traditional deities like Tonantzin continued to be the object of Nahua veneration, and he criticized syncretism as a false path to faith. Historians read the legend of Juan Diego as a social device purposely adopted by indigenous community leaders, perhaps the *caciques* themselves, to blend ancient Aztec cult practices with Christian doctrine. Forms of worship evolved that honored both conceptions of a holy mother. Similar transformations were relatively common throughout New Spain, sometimes with the tacit support of the mendicant orders.[88]

Religious assimilation operated as a cultural bridge to reconcile past and present. Church festivals dedicated to such transformations became a fundamental form of social, religious, and political expression. Scheduled in accordance with the Christian calendar, festivals were coordinated with markets and other traditional forms of exchange, just as they had been in pre-Hispanic times. Long after ceasing to serve the aims of empire, the Aztec gods have passed from the emperors into the hands of the people, and have taken on new significance. Like the gods of classical antiquity, their afterlife represents the dynamic interplay between tradition and innovation that shapes the modern contours of the Mexican nation.

XXV | Nude Woman, found in Texcoco | 1450–1521 | Basalt | H 154 × W 51 × D 32 cm (61½ × 20½ × 13 in.) | Museo Nacional de Antropología, Mexico City | 10–81543

Nicknamed the Venus of Texcoco, this remarkable figure is the only known life-sized statue of a female nude in Aztec sculpture. A rectangular slot in the chest would have held a "heart" of greenstone. Together with the eyes inlaid with shell and obsidian, the image was believed to be endowed with a life force. The statue would have been adorned with a wig, headdress, and garments for various feasts held throughout the year.

XXVI | Eagle Cuauhxicalli, found in the Templo Mayor, Mexico City | about 1500 | Basalt | H 59 × W 112 × D 107 cm (23¼ × 44⅛ × 42⅛ in.) | Museo del Templo Mayor, Mexico City | 10–252747

Emperor of birds, the eagle is a fundamental symbol often associated with the loftiest ideals of spiritual and political power. For the Aztecs the eagle was the divine messenger of the sun, which delivered to the god Tonatiuh his daily food of human hearts. The hearts were transformed into an ethereal gift once cremated in the basin on the eagle's back. Certain religious practitioners were also believed to be able to transform themselves into eagles in order to fly to the distant worlds of the ancestors. Cihuacoatl, the patron goddess of healers and midwives, was also invoked as a white eagle.

XXVII | Roman Eagle | AD 100–300 | Bronze | H 104.2 × W 78.7 × D 76.2 cm (41 × 31 × 30 in.) | J. Paul Getty Museum, Malibu | 72.AB.151

Monumental bronze eagles such as this often accompanied imperial portraits or sculptures of the Roman god Jupiter. As an emblem of ancient Rome, the spread-winged golden eagle has its roots in the republican army of Marius, who adopted it as a heraldic standard for each division of his army. Later it served as a symbol of authority throughout the Roman Empire.

A pair of effigies was excavated in the House of the Eagles, which may have been dedicated to a special military order, the members of which wore a *tlahuiztli* (fitted body garment) adorned with eagle feathers. Warfare was a fundamental means of social promotion in Aztec society and all young men were expected to participate. For each war captive they brought home to sacrifice at the Templo Mayor, they were handsomely rewarded with gifts from the emperor. After presenting six captives and earning an array of magnificent battle dress, a warrior was either eligible for promotion to the rank of general or entitled to join an elite order of combat veterans.

XXIX | Xipe Totec, found in Tepexi el Viejo | About 1500 | Terracotta and pigment | H 96.8 × W 31.8 × D 21.6 cm (38⅛ × 12½ × 8½ in.) | Museo Regional de Puebla | 10–203061

Xipe Totec (Flayed God) is portrayed as a priest wearing a human skin. The cult of Xipe Totec had its roots in ancient Mesoamerican ceremonies, in which warfare was conceptually linked to agricultural fertility. Festivals dedicated to the god featured gladiatorial combats in which ranking noble captives were forced to defend themselves against two pairs of warriors dressed as eagles and jaguars. In reality, the combat was a ritual execution as the warriors wielded the razor-edged *macuahuitl*, a wooden sword fixed with obsidian blades, while the captive was only armed with a simple wooden club. After the captive was so badly injured that he could no longer fight, he was sacrificed, and his flayed skin was worn by a priest.

XXX | Temple Model | About 1500 | Terracotta | H 32.2 × W 16.8 × D 19.5 cm (12¾ × 6⅝ × 7⅝ in.) | Museo Nacional de Antropología, Mexico City | 10–223673

Because Aztec religious precincts were largely dismantled to construct the colonial cities of New Spain, miniature models of metropolitan temples have been invaluable to archaeologists in reconstructing ancient architecture. Probably intended for household altars, replicas of pyramids first occur during the period of Aztec domination and are related to the elite urban cults. The series of human skulls may identify this as a shrine dedicated to Tezcatlipoca. Decorating the roof are conch shell tiles, similar examples of which were excavated at the Templo Mayor. Conch trumpets were used to summon people for major festivals, and the shell is associated with both the underworld and fertility.

XXXI | Sacrificial Stone | About 1500 **|** Greenstone **|** H 48.3 × D 83.8 cm (19 × 33 in.) **|** The Louise and Walter Arensburg Collection, 1950. Philadelphia Museum of Art **|** 1950–134–403

This outstanding example of a sacrificial stone is thematically related to the famous Aztec calendar stone. According to legend, the fifth and present age, or "sun"—symbolized by the sign 4 Earthquake carved on the stone's upper surface—was brought into being by a humble and sickly god who sacrificed himself at the summit of a pyramid at Teotihuacan. Once transfigured as Tonatiuh, he refused to move across the sky without offerings of the sacred sustenance that energized him—human hearts. The gods therefore invented warfare to "feed" the sun god and insure that he would rise each morning to bring life-giving warmth to the earth. It is difficult to conceive of a more dramatic myth to support a state's imperial mandate of conquest.

Feasts, festivals, and markets were coordinated throughout the empire in accordance with synchronized calendars. On Gemelli Careri's schematic diagram, the symbols of the outer band represent a fifty-two-year cycle, corresponding to the European concept of a century. Symbols in the inner band represent the principal feasts held every twenty days in Tenochtitlan's central ceremonial precinct.

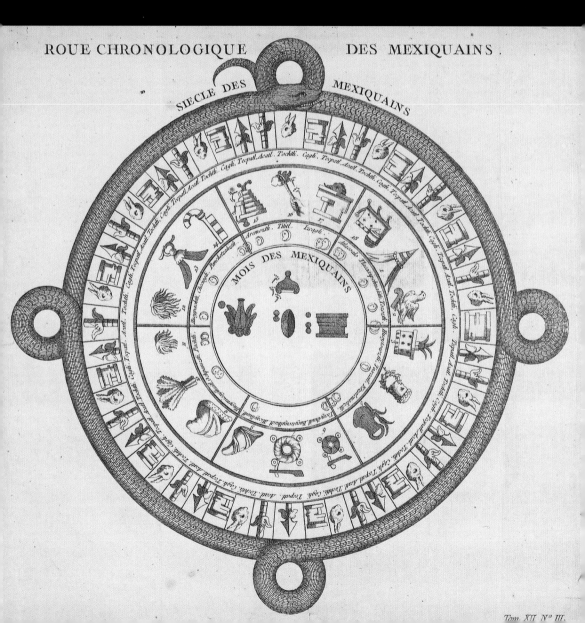

XXXIII | Ehecatl-Quetzalcoatl, found in Calixtlahuaca | About 1500 | Basalt and pigment | H 176 × W 56 × D 50 cm (69¼ × 22 × 19⅝ in.) | Museo de Antropología e Historia del Estado de México, Toluca | 10–109262

Recovered from the debris of the circular temple in Calixtlahuaca (Matlazinca), the deity appears in his guise as the wind god Ehecatl, identifiable by a mask of a muscovy duck, the "royal duck" of the Aztecs. Highly refined in the execution of the human form, it is characteristic of Mexica metropolitan style. Such works are relatively rare outside the Basin of Mexico and this piece stands apart from local styles of relief carving that predominated in the Toluca Valley.

XXXIV | The Conquest of Mexico | Anonymous | About 1630–1700 | Oil on canvas | H 1.87 × W 4.88 m (6 ft. 1½ in. × 16 ft. ½ in.) |
Collection of the Banco Nacional de México, Mexico City | Pl. 0387

XXXV | Fertility Goddess, found in the Toluca-Guerrero region | 1250–1521 | Cedarwood and shell | H 39.5 × W 15 × D 10.2 cm (15½ × 5⅞ × 4 in.) | Museo Nacional de Antropología, Mexico City | 10–74751

Wooden cult figures are rare archaeological survivals but were once common objects. Despite the Spanish authorities' determination to eradicate Aztec deities, this figure was still the object of active worship within the cave where it was discovered in the nineteenth century. This spectacular image depicts a seminude woman in a plain wraparound skirt. Wearing the coiffure of a married woman, her hair has been separated into two coils and bound up around the top of her head. She holds her breasts in a maternal gesture of fecundity. Her enlarged head, hands, and feet are reflective of the Nahua-Mixteca style of southern Mexico.

Notes

1. Davíd Carrasco, ed., *The History of the Conquest of New Spain by Bernal Díaz del Castillo* (Albuquerque: University of New Mexico Press, 2009), 300.

2. Ibid., 304–305.

3. Patricia Seed, *Ceremonies of Possession in Europe's Conquest of the New World, 1492–1640* (Cambridge: Cambridge University Press, 1995), 57–68.

4. Richard F. Townsend, *The Aztecs* (New York: Thames and Hudson, 2000), 53–65.

5. John M. D. Pohl, *Exploring Mesoamerica* (New York: Oxford University Press, 1999), 150–161.

6. John M. D. Pohl, "Creation Stories, Hero Cults, and Alliance Building: Postclassic Confederacies of Central and Southern Mexico from A.D. 1150–1458," in *The Postclassic Mesoamerican World*, eds. Michael Smith and Frances Berdan (Salt Lake City: University of Utah Press, 2003), 62–63.

7. Richard F. Townsend, *The Aztecs* (New York: Thames and Hudson, 2000), 64–70.

8. Michael Smith, *The Aztecs* (Oxford: Blackwell Publishing, 2003), 37–55.

9. Diego Durán, *The History of the Indies of New Spain*, translated, annotated, and with an introduction by Doris Heyden (Norman: University of Oklahoma Press, 1994), 387–393.

10. John H. Elliot, "The Overthrow of Moctezuma and His Empire," in *Moctezuma: Aztec Ruler*, eds. Colin McEwan and Leonardo López Luján (London: British Museum Press, 2009), 218–233.

11. Marie Tanner, *The Last Descendant of Aeneas: The Hapsburgs and the Mythic Image of the Emperor* (New Haven: Yale University Press, 1993), 112–114.

12. Jugate Portraits of Emperor Charles V and King Philip II of Spain (obverse) and Empress Isabella (reverse), 1550. New York: The Metropolitan Museum of Art, inv. 38.150.9.

13. Kelley Helmstutler Di Dio, "Pompeo Leoni and His Collection in Madrid," *Journal of the History of Collections* 18 no. 2 (2006): 137–167, esp. 151ff.

14. Marie Tanner, *The Last Descendant of Aeneas: The Hapsburgs and the Mythic Image of the Emperor* (New Haven: Yale University Press, 1993), 113 and 155, fig. 80.

Thomas B. F. Cummins, *Through a Looking Glass Darkly: Titian, Serlio, Iciar, and Hercules in the Americas; Brazilians, Peruvians, Aztecs and Zemis in Europe*, conference paper in "The Places of Art: A Symposium in Honor of Charles Talbot," Trinity University, San Antonio, TX, April 17, 2008.

15. Anthony Grafton, *What Was History? The Art of History in Early Modern Europe* (Cambridge: Cambridge University Press, 2007), 70–100.

16. Sabine MacCormack, "Limits of Understanding: Perceptions of Greco-Roman and Amerindian Paganism in Early Modern Europe," in *America in European Consciousness, 1493–1750*, ed. Karen O. Kupperman (Williamsburg, VA: University of North Carolina Press, 1995), 79–129.

17. David A. Lupher, *Romans in a New World: Classical Models in Sixteenth-Century Spanish America* (Ann Arbor: University of Michigan Press, 2003), 68–82.

18. John M. D. Pohl and Charles M. Robinson, *Aztecs and Conquistadores: The Spanish Invasion and the Collapse of the Aztec Empire* (Oxford: Osprey Publishing, 2005), 95–104, 110–123.

19. Vitoria, as translated and quoted in David A. Lupher, *Romans in a New World: Classical Models in Sixteenth-Century Spanish America* (Ann Arbor: University of Michigan Press, 2003), 73–74.

20. David A. Lupher, *Romans in a New World: Classical Models in Sixteenth-Century Spanish America* (Ann Arbor: University of Michigan Press, 2003), 103–149.

21. Serge Gruzinski, *The Aztecs: Rise and Fall of an Empire* (New York: Harry N. Abrams, 1992).

Benjamin Keen, *The Aztec Image in Western Thought* (New Brunswick, NJ: Rutgers University Press, 1991), 73–74.

22. Luis N. D'Olwer and Howard F. Cline, "Bernardino de Sahagún, 1499–1590," in *Handbook of Middle American Indians*, Robert Wauchope, general ed., vol.13.2, *Guide to Ethnohistorical Sources*, ed. Howard F. Cline and John B. Glass (Austin: University of Texas Press, 1973), 186–239.

J. Jorge Klor de Alva, Henry B. Nicholson, and Eloise Quiñones Keber, eds., *The Work of Bernardino de Sahagún: Pioneer Ethnographer of Sixteenth-Century Aztec Mexico* (Albany: Institute for Mesoamerican Studies, State University of New York, 1988).

23. Henry B. Nicholson, "Introduction," in *Primeros Memoriales*, paleography of Nahuatl text and English translation by Thelma D. Sullivan. Completed and revised with additions by Henry B. Nicholson et al. (Norman: University of Oklahoma Press, 1997), 3–14.

24. Bernardino de Sahagún, *Primeros Memoriales*, paleography of Nahuatl text and English translation by Thelma D. Sullivan. Completed and revised with additions by Henry B. Nicholson et al. (Norman: University of Oklahoma Press, 1997), 93–94.

25. Ellen T. Baird, *The Drawings of Sahagún's Primeros Memoriales: Structure and Style* (Norman: University of Oklahoma Press, 1993), fig. 29.

26. Serge Gruzinski, *The Aztecs: Rise and Fall of an Empire* (New York: Harry N. Abrams, 1992), 64–77.

27. Bernardino de Sahagún, *Historia general de las cosas de Nueva España*, ed. Ángel María Garibay, 4 vols. (Mexico City: Biblioteca Porrua, 1956), I:29.

28. Andrew Laird, "The *Aeneid* from the Aztecs to the Dark Virgin: Vergil, Native Tradition and Latin Poetry in Colonial Mexico from Sahagún's *Memoriales* (1563) to

Villerías' *Guadelupe* (1724)," in *A Companion to Vergil's Aeneid and its Tradition. Blackwell Companions to the Ancient World*, ed. Joseph Farrell and Michael C. J. Putnam (Malden, MA, and Oxford: John Wiley & Sons, 2010), 217–233.

29. Michael W. Mathes, *The America's First Academic Library: Santa Cruz de Tlatelolco* (Sacramento: California State Library Foundation, 1985). David A. Lupher, *Romans in a New World: Classical Models in Sixteenth-Century Spanish America* (Ann Arbor: University of Michigan Press, 2003), 231–233.

30. Andrew Laird, "Latin in Cuauhtémoc's Shadow: Humanism and the Politics of Language in Mexico after the Conquest," in *Latinity and Alterity in the Early Modern Period*, eds. Yasmin Haskell and Juanita Feros Ruys (Tempe: Arizona Center for Medieval and Renaissance Studies, 2009), 180–181.

31. Arthur J. O. Anderson and Charles E. Dibble, *The War of Conquest: How It Was Waged Here in Mexico* (Salt Lake City: University of Utah Press, 1978), 12–15.

32. Camilla Townsend, "Burying the White Gods: New Perspectives on the Conquest of Mexico," *The American Historical Review* 108 (2003): 659–687.

33. Felipe Fernández-Armesto, "'Aztec' Auguries and Memories of the Conquest of Mexico," *Renaissance Studies* 6 (1992): 287–305, esp. 292–293.

34. H. B. Nicholson, "Religion in Pre-Hispanic Central Mexico," in *Handbook of Middle American Indians*, Robert Wauchope, general ed., vol.13.2, *Guide to Ethnohistorical Sources*, eds. Howard F. Cline and John B. Glass (Austin: University of Texas Press, 1973), 409.

35. Ibid., 408–410.

36. Jane Webster, "Creolizing the Roman Provinces," *American Journal of Archaeology* 105 (2001): 209–225.

37. John M. D. Pohl, *The Politics of Symbolism in the Mixtec Codices* (Nashville, TN: Vanderbilt University Publications in Anthropology 46, 1994), 23–41.

38. Richard F. Townsend, "State and Cosmos in the Art of Tenochtitlan," *Studies in Pre-Columbian Art and Archaeology* 20 (Washington, DC: Dumbarton Oaks and the Trustees for Harvard University, 1979), 27–28.

Arild Hvidtfeldt, *Teotl and Ixiptlatli: Some Central Conceptions in Ancient Mexican Religion: With a General Introduction on Cult and Myth* (Copenhagen: Munksgaard, 1958).

39. Eulogio Guzmán, *Sculpting Imperialism? The Diverse Expression of Local Cults and Corporate Identity in the "Two-Tufted" Figure at the Templo Mayor* (Ph.D. dissertation, Department of Art History, University of California Los Angeles, 2004).

Leonardo López Luján, *The Offerings of the Templo Mayor of Tenochtitlan*, translated by Bernard R. Ortiz de Montellano and Thelma Ortiz de Montellano (Albuquerque: University of New Mexico Press, 2005).

40. Henry B. Nicholson, "Polychrome on Aztec Sculpture," in *Painted Architecture and Polychrome Monumental Sculpture in Mesoamerica: A Symposium at Dumbarton Oaks*, 10–11 October 1981 (Washington, DC:

Dumbarton Oaks and the Trustees for Harvard University, 1985), 145–171.

41. H. B. Nicholson, "Religion in Pre-Hispanic Central Mexico," in *Handbook of Middle American Indians*, Robert Wauchope, general ed., vol.13.2, *Guide to Ethnohistorical Sources*, ed. Howard F. Cline and John B. Glass (Austin: University of Texas Press, 1973), 420–421.

42. Alfredo López Austin, "Hombre-Dios: Religión y política en el mundo náhuatl," *Serie de Cultura Náhuatl*, monografías 15 (Mexico: Universidad Nacional Autónoma, Instituto de Investigaciones Históricas, 1973).

43. Elizabeth Hill Boone, *Incarnations of the Aztec Supernatural: The Image of Huitzilopochtli in Mexico and Europe*, Transactions of the American Philosophical Society, vol. 79.2 (Philadelphia, PA: American Philosophical Society, 1989), 70–83.

Peter Mason, *The Lives of Images* (London: Reaktion Books, 2001), 101–147.

44. Lynn Hunt, Margaret Jacob, and Wijnand Mijnhardt, eds., *Bernard Picart and the First Global Vision of Religion* (Los Angeles: Getty Research Institute, 2010).

45. *Jupiter* (1591), engraving by Hendrik Goltzius (Netherlandish, 1558–1617), after the Eight Deities suite by Polidoro da Caravaggio. Los Angeles: Research Library, the Getty Research Institute, 2001.PR.20*.

46. Verónica Gutiérrez, "Quetzalcoatl's Enlightened City: A Close Reading of Bernard Picart's Engraving of Chollopan/Cholula," in *Bernard Picart and the First Global Vision of Religion*, eds. Lynn Hunt, Margaret Jacob, and Wijnand Mijnhardt (Los Angeles: Getty Research Institute, 2010), 251–270.

47. Stephen Greenblatt, *Marvelous Possessions: The Wonder of the New World* (Chicago: University of Chicago Press, 1992).

48. Cecelia F. Klein, "Wild Woman in Colonial Mexico: An Encounter of European and Aztec Concepts of the Other," in *Reframing the Renaissance: Visual Culture in Europe and Latin America 1450–1650*, ed. Claire Farago (New Haven: Yale University Press, 1995), 245–263.

Eadem, "A New Interpretation of the Aztec Statue Called Coatlicue, 'Snakes-her-Skirt,'" *Ethnohistory* 55, no. 2 (2008): 229–250.

49. Trevor Murphy, *Pliny the Elder's* Natural History: *The Empire in the Encyclopedia* (New York: Oxford University Press, 2004), 88–90.

Margaret T. Hodgen, *Early Anthropology in the Sixteenth and Seventeenth Centuries* (Philadelphia: University of Pennsylvania Press, 1964), 17–48.

50. Cecelia F. Klein, "Wild Woman in Colonial Mexico: An Encounter of European and Aztec Concepts of the Other," in *Reframing the Renaissance: Visual Culture in Europe and Latin America 1450–1650*, ed. Claire Farago (New Haven: Yale University Press, 1995), 245–263.

51. Ibid., 263.

52. Antonio de León y Gama, *Descripción histórica y cronológica de las piedras que con ocasión del nuevo empedrado que se está formando en la plaza principal de*

México, se hallaron en ella el año de 1790… (Mexico: Don Felipe de Zúniga y Ontiveros, 1792).

53. Khristaan Villela and Mary Ellen Miller, eds., *The Calendar Stone* (Los Angeles: Getty Research Institute, 2010).

54. Leonardo López Luján, "Noticias de Herculano," *Arqueología Mexicana* 90 (2008): 74–80.

55. Felipe Solís Olguín, "Adventures and Misadventures of the National Museum of Anthropology's Collections," in *National Museum of Anthropology Mexico City*, ed. Felipe Solís Olguín (New York: Harry N. Abrams, 2003), 59–61.

56. Emily Umberger, *Aztec Sculptures, Hieroglyphs and History* (Ph.D. dissertation, Columbia University, 1981).

Esther Pasztory, *Aztec Art* (New York: Harry N. Abrams, 1983), 165–168.

57. Jean Seznec, *The Survival of the Pagan Gods: The Mythological Tradition and Its Place in Renaissance Humanism and Art* (Princeton: Princeton University Press, 1953).

58. Simon Keay, "Recent Archaeological Work in Roman Iberia (1990–2002)," *Journal of Roman Studies* 93 (2003): 148, nn. 13–16.

59. Richard Kagan, *Cities of the Golden Age: The Views of Anton van den Wyngaerde* (Berkeley and Los Angeles: University of California Press, 1989), 335–340.

Margarita Díaz-Andreu, G. Mora, & J. Cortadella, *Diccionario Histórico de la Arqueología en España* (siglos xv–xx), (Madrid: Marcial Pons, 2009).

60. Gloria Mora, "The Image of Rome in Spain: Scholars, Artists, and Architects in Italy During the 16th to 18th Century," in *Images of Rome: Perceptions of Ancient Rome in Europe and the United States in the Modern Age*, ed. Richard Hingley, *Journal of Roman Archaeology*, suppl. 44, (2001), 23–55.

61. Felipe Solís Olguín, "The Art of the Aztec Era," in *The Aztec World*, eds. Elizabeth M. Brumfiel and Gary M. Feinman (New York: Harry N. Abrams, 2008), 171–178.

62. Henry B. Nicholson, "Polychrome on Aztec Sculpture," in *Painted Architecture and Polychrome Monumental Sculpture in Mesoamerica: A Symposium at Dumbarton Oaks*, 10–11 October 1981 (Washington, DC: Dumbarton Oaks and the Trustees for Harvard University, 1985),145–171.

63. Rudolf Wittkower, "Eagle and Serpent: A Study in the Migration of Symbols," *Journal of the Warburg Institute* 2 no. 4 (1939): 293–325.

Peter Mason, *The Lives of Images* (London: Reaktion Books, 2001), 11–13.

64. Susan E. Alcock, Terence N. D'Altroy, Kathleen D. Morrison, and Carla M. Sinopoli, eds., *Empires: Perspectives from Archaeology and History* (Cambridge: Cambridge University Press, 2001), 1–9.

Thomas J. Barfield, "The Shadow Empires: Imperial State Formation along the Chinese Nomad Frontier," in *Empires: Perspectives from Archaeology and History*, eds. Susan E. Alcock, Terence N. D'Altroy, Kathleen D. Morrison, and Carla M. Sinopoli (Cambridge: Cambridge University Press, 2001), 29.

65. Kathleen D. Morrison, "Sources, Approaches, and Definitions," in *Empires: Perspectives from Archaeology and History*, eds. Susan E. Alcock, Terence N. D'Altroy, Kathleen D. Morrison, and Carla M. Sinopoli (Cambridge: Cambridge University Press, 2001), 3.

66. Chris Gosden, *Archaeology and Colonialism* (Cambridge: Cambridge University Press, 2004), 72–80.

Claire L. Lyons and John K. Papadopoulos, *The Archaeology of Colonialism* (Los Angeles: Getty Research Institute, 2002), 12–13.

67. Richard C. Beacham, *Spectacle Entertainments of Early Imperial Rome* (New Haven: Yale University Press, 1995) 49–74.

Mary Beard, *The Roman Triumph* (Cambridge, MA: Harvard University Press, 2009), 7–41.

68. T. J. Luce, "Livy, Augustus, and the Forum Augustum," in *Between Republic and Empire*, ed. Kurt Raaflaub and Mark Toher (Berkeley and Los Angeles: University of California Press, 1993), 123–138.

69. Joseph Geiger, *The First Hall of Fame: A Study of the Statues in the Forum of Augustus* (Leiden, Boston: Brill, 2008).

70. Davíd Carrasco, ed., *The History of the Conquest of New Spain by Bernal Díaz del Castillo* (Albuquerque: University of New Mexico Press, 2009), 156.

71. Carlos Javier González González, "Xipe Tótec, tlacaxipehualiztli y el legado mexica: La transferencia simbólica del poder," in *Símbolos de poder en Mesoamérica*, coordination and introduction by Guilhem Olivier (Mexico: Universidad Nacional Autónoma de México, Instituto de Investigaciones Históricas, Instituto de Investigaciones Antropológicas, 2008), 350–371.

72. Eduardo Matos Moctezuma, *The Great Temple of the Aztecs: Treasures of Tenochtitlan* (London: Thames and Hudson, 1988).

73. Eduardo Matos Moctezuma and Felipe Solís Olguín, eds., *Aztecs* (London: Royal Academy of Arts, 2002).

Felipe Solís Olguín, "The Art of the Aztec Era," in *The Aztec World*, eds. Elizabeth M. Brumfiel and Gary M. Feinman (New York: Harry N. Abrams, 2008), 153–178.

74. Eduardo Matos Moctezuma, *The Great Temple of the Aztecs: Treasures of Tenochtitlan* (London: Thames and Hudson, 1988), 40–43.

75. Bernardino de Sahagún, *Florentine Codex: General History of the Things of New Spain*, translated and ed. Charles E. Dibble and Arthur J. O. Anderson, 13 vols. (Santa Fe, NM: School of American Research, 1950–1982), III:3–4.

76. Ibid., 4–5.

77. John M. D. Pohl, *Aztec Warrior: AD 1325–1521* (Oxford: Osprey Publishing, 2001), 48–49.

78. Alfredo López Austin and Leonardo López Luján, "Aztec Human Sacrifice," in *The Aztec World*, eds. Elizabeth M. Brumfiel and Gary M. Feinman (New York: Harry N. Abrams), 137–152.

79. John M. D. Pohl, *Aztec Warrior: AD 1325–1521* (Oxford: Osprey Publishing, 2001), 50.

80. Eduardo Matos Moctezuma and Felipe Solís Olguín,

El calendario Azteca y otros monumentos solares (México: Instituto Nacional de Antropología e Historia, 2004), 110–119.

81. Richard F. Townsend, *The Aztecs* (New York: Thames and Hudson, 2000), 108.

82. Michael Smith, "Calixtlahuaca, organización de un centro urbano postclásico: Informe Técnico Parcial, temporada de 2006," report submitted to the Consejo de Arqueología, Instituto Nacional de Antropología e Historia, Mexico City, 2006.

Emily Umberger, "Historia del arte e Imperio Azteca: La evidencia de las esculturas," *Revista Española de Antropología Americana* 37 (2006), 165–202.

83. Simon J. Keay, *Roman Spain* (Berkeley and Los Angeles: University of California Press, 1988), 72.

Leonard A. Curchin, *Roman Spain: Conquest and Assimilation* (New York: Routledge, 1991), 55.

84. Simon Keay, "Recent Archaeological Work in Roman Iberia (1990–2002)," *Journal of Roman Studies* 93 (2003): 146–211, esp. 163–189.

Andrew Wallace-Hadrill, *Rome's Cultural Revolution* (Cambridge: Cambridge University Press, 2005), 63–64.

85. Linda A. Curcio-Nagy, *The Great Festivals of Colonial Mexico City: Performing Power and Identity* (Albuquerque: University of New Mexico Press, 2004).

86. Toribio de Benavente Motolinía, *History of the Indians of New Spain*, ed. Elizabeth A. Foster (Berkeley: The Cortés Society, 1950), 101–120.

87. Margaret A. Jackson and Rebecca P. Brienen, *Visions of Empire: Picturing the Conquest in Colonial Mexico* (Coral Gables, FL: Lowe Art Museum, University of Miami, 2003).

Elisa Vargaslugo, "Images of the Conquest in Seventeenth-Century Art: Two Visions," in *Images of the Natives in the Art of New Spain: 16th to 18th Centuries*, eds. Elisa Vargaslugo et al. (Mexico: Banamex, 2005), 95–123.

88. Susan Schroeder and Stafford Poole, eds., *Religion in New Spain* (Albuquerque: University of New Mexico Press, 2007), 1–11.

Pronunciation Guide to Frequently Used Aztec Names and Terms

Acolhua
(*Ah-KOHL-waa*)

Ahuitzotl
(*Ah-WEET-zote*)

Anecuyotl
(*Ah-nay-KOO-yoat*)

Apapaxco
(*Ah-pah-PAHSH-ko*)

Azcapotzalco
(*Oz-kaa-poat-ZAHL-koh*)

Axayacatl
(*Ah-sha-YAA-kot*)

Calixtlahuaca
(*Kaa-leesh-tlaa-WAA-kaa*)

Centeotl
(*Sen-TAY-oat*)

Chalchiuhtlicue
(*Chahl-chee-oot-LEE-kuay*)

Chapultepec
(*Chaa-POOL-tay-peck*)

Chicomecoatl
(*Chee-koh-may-KOH-ot*)

Chicomexochitl
(*Chee-koh-may-SHOW-cheet*)

Chicomoztoc
(*Chee-koh-MOSE-tok*)

Chinampa
(*Chee-NOM-paa*)

Cihuacoatl
(*See-wha-KOH-ot*)

Coatepec
(*Ko-AH-tay-peck*)

Coatlicue
(*Ko-ah-TLEE-kway*)

Coyolxauhqui
(*Koh-yol-SHAUH-key*)

Cuauhtemoc
(*Koh-wow-TAY-mok*)

Cuauhtitlan
(*Koh-wow-teet-LON*)

Cuauhtlatoatzin
(*Koh-wow-tlaa-toe-OT-zeen*)

Cuauhxicalli
(*Koh-wow-she-KAA-lee*)

Cuitlahuac
(*Kwee-TLAA-wok*)

Culhuacan
(*Kool-WAA-kon*)

Ehecatl
(*Eh-HAY-kot*)

Huextozinco
(*Way-shoat-ZEEN-ko*)

Huey tlatoani
(*Way-tlaa-toe-AH-nee*)

Huey tlatoque
(*Way-tlaa-TOE-kay*)

Huitzilopochtli
(*Weet-zeel-low-POCH-tlee*)

Ixmiquilpan
(*Eesh-mee-KWEEL-pon*)

Ixptla
(*EESH-p-tlaa*)

Ixtlilxochitl
(*Eesh-leel-SHOW-cheet*)

Izcoatl
(*Eez-KOH-ot*)

Macehualtin
(*Mah-say-WAHL-teen*)

Macuahuitl
(*Mah-koo-AH-weet*)

Matlazinca
(*Mah-tlaa-ZEEN-kaa*)

Maxtla
(*MOSH-tlaa*)

Maxtlatl
(*MOSH-tlot*)

Mayahuel
(*Maa-yaa-WELL*)

Mexica
(*May-SHEE-kaa*)

Mictlantecuhtli
(*Mick-tlon-tay-KOO-tlee*)

Mixteca
(*Meesh-TAY-kaa*)

Motecuhzoma
(*Moe-tay-koo-ZOH-maa*)

Nahual
(*NAA-wall*)

Nahuatl
(*NAA-wot*)

Octli
(*OAK-tlee*)

Popocatepetl
(*Poh-poh-kaa-TAY-pet*)

Quechquemitl
(*katch-KAY-meet*)

Quetzalcoatl
(*Kate-zahl-KO-ot*)

Talcathedani
(*Tall-kah-thay-DA-nee*)

Tecuhtli
(*Tay-KOO-tlee*)

Tehuehuelli
(*Tay-way-WAY-lee*)

Tenochca
  (*Tay-NOACH-kaa*)

Tenochtitlan
  (*Tay-noach-TEET-lon*)

Teotihuacan
  (*Tay-oh-tee-WHA-kon*)

Teotl
  (*TAY-oat*)

Tepepulco
  (*Tay-pay-PULL-koh*)

Tepeyac
  (*Tay-pay-YOCK*)

Tepeyolotl
  (*Tay-pay-YOH-loat*)

Tepoztecatl
  (*Tay-pose-TAY-kot*)

Tepoztlan
  (*Tay-pose-TLON*)

Tetecuhtin
  (*Tay-tay-KOO-teen*)

Teteoinnan
  (*Tay-tay-oh-EE-nahn*)

Texcoco
  (*Taysh-KO-ko*)

Tezcatlipoca
  (*Tays-kot-tlee-POH-kaa*)

Tezcatzoncatl
  (*Tays-kot-ZONE-kot*)

Tilmatli
  (*Teel-MOT-tlee*)

Tizoc
  (*TEE-zok*)

Tlacaxipehualiztli
  (*Tlaa-kaa-she-pay-wahl-LEEZ-tlee*)

Tlacopan
  (*Tlaa-KOH-pon*)

Tlahuiztli
  (*Tlaa-WHEEZ-tlee*)

Tlalmanalco
  (*Tlal-mah-NAL-ko*)

Tlaloc
  (*TLAA-lock*)

Tlalocan
  (*Tlaa-LOH-kon*)

Tlalpan
  (*TLAAL-pon*)

Tlaltecuhtli
  (*Tlaal-tay-KOO-tlee*)

Tlatelolco
  (*Tlaa-tay-LOHL-ko*)

Tlaquimilolli
  (*Tlaa-kwee-mee-LOH-lee*)

Tlaxcala
  (*Tlash-KAH-la*)

Tlaxcalteca
  (*Tlahsh-kahl-TAY-ka*)

Tonantzin
  (*Toe-NONT-zeen*)

Tonatiuh
  (*Toe-naa-TEE-you*)

Toxcatl
  (*TOSH-cot*)

Tzitzimime
  (*Zeet-zee-MEE-may*)

Tzitzimitl
  (*Zeet-ZEE-meet*)

Tzompantli
  (*Zom-PON-tlee*)

Xicolli
  (*She-KOH-lee*)

Xipe Totec
  (*She-pay TOE-teck*)

Xiuhtecuhtli
  (*She-you-tay-KOOT-tlee*)

Xochipilli
  (*Show-chee-PEE-lee*)

Xochiquetzal
  (*Show-chee-KATE-zahl*)

Xocoyotzin
  (*Show-ko-YOAT-zeen*)

Yohualtecuhtli
  (*Yoh-wahl-tay-KOOT-lee*)

Index

Illustrations are indicated by entries and page numbers in *italics*. Plates are indicated by Pl. following the page number.